William Golding
Revised Edition

Twayne's English Authors Series

Kinley E. Roby, Editor

Northeastern University

TEAS 57

WILLIAM GOLDING
(1911–   )
Photograph by Jerry Bauer
Reproduced courtesy of Farrar, Straus and Giroux

William Golding

Revised Edition

By Bernard F. Dick

Fairleigh Dickinson University

Twayne Publishers
A Division of G. K. Hall & Co. • *Boston*

60990

William Golding
Revised Edition

Bernard F. Dick

Copyright © 1987 by G. K. Hall & Co.
All Rights Reserved
Published by Twayne Publishers
A Division of G. K. Hall & Co.
70 Lincoln Street
Boston, Massachusetts 02111

Copyediting supervised by Lewis DeSimone
Book production by Marne B. Sultz
Book design by Barbara Anderson

First Printing

Typeset in 11 pt. Garamond
by Compset, Inc., Beverly, Massachusetts

Printed on permanent/durable acid-free paper
and bound in the United States of America

Library of Congress Cataloging in Publication Data

Dick, Bernard F.
    William Golding.

    (Twayne's English authors series ; TEAS 57)
    Bibliography: p. 162
    Includes index.
    1. Golding, William, 1911–   —Criticism and
interpretation.   I. Title.   II. Series.
PR6013.035Z6   1987   823'.914   86-14857
ISBN 0-8057-6925-0

For Anita and Katherine

Contents

About the Author

Bernard F. Dick, who was born in Scranton, Pennsylvania, received his B.A. in classics and literature from the University of Scranton in 1957 and his Ph.D. in classics from Fordham University in 1962. He taught classics at Iona College from 1961 to 1970, serving as department chair from 1967 to 1970. Since 1970, he has been a member of the Department of English and Comparative Literature at Fairleigh Dickinson University where he served as department chair of the Teaneck campus from 1973 to 1979. Currently a professor of English and Comparative literature, he also regularly teaches courses in film criticism and history. His first book was the first edition of *William Golding* (1967). He has also written two books in Twayne's Filmmakers Series: *Billy Wilder* (1980) and *Joseph L. Mankiewicz* (1983). Other books include *The Hellenism of Mary Renault* (1972), *The Apostate Angel: A Critical Study of Gore Vidal* (1974), *Anatomy of Film* (1978), *Hellman in Hollywood* (1982), and *The Star-Spangled Screen: The American World War II Film* (1985). His articles have appeared in *Georgia Review, Sewanee Review, Southern Quarterly, Literature and Film Quarterly, Comparative Literature,* and *College English.* His book reviews have been published in *Contemporary Literature, Modern Drama, World Literature Today,* and *Saturday Review.* A member of the editorial board of the *Quarterly Review of Film Studies,* he is married to Katherine Restaino, Dean of St. Peter's College at Englewood Cliffs, New Jersey.

Preface

The 1967 edition of this book ended with a question: "Where does one go after becoming Aeschylean?" The question had been posed because Golding considers himself an Aeschylean novelist, one who is no more satisfied with a surface examination of human behavior than Aeschylus was. In his great trilogy, the *Oresteia*, Aeschylus traced an ancestral curse back a generation to account for the tragedy that befell the family of Agamemnon.

That Golding calls himself Aeschylean is important for another reason. Roughly from the end of World War II to the early 1960s, Golding limited his reading largely to the Greeks. *The Spire* (1964), the last novel discussed in the 1967 edition, ended the first phase of his career; in that novel, Golding brought the classical spirit to a level unique in modern fiction. To exceed it, he felt, would be risking hybris, and Golding is too much of a classicist to tempt the gods.

"Where does one go after becoming Aeschylean?" is the question the revised edition attempts to answer by juxtaposing the early and later Golding to create as complete a portrait of the writer as possible—from *Poems* (1934) to *An Egyptian Journal* (1985).

The revised edition of *William Golding* is more than a continuation of the first. The material that appeared in the 1967 edition has been substantially rewritten, especially in the case of *Lord of the Flies*, *The Inheritors*, and *The Spire*; the Dantean influence on *Pincher Martin* and *Free Fall* has been expanded. It was especially important to rewrite the chapter on *Lord of the Flies*, which in the late 1960s moved out of the colleges into the high schools. *Lord of the Flies* will probably always be Golding's most popular novel; it was certainly a factor in his winning the Nobel Prize. The revised edition of *William Golding* offers new insights into the work to show how multileveled it is.

The basic premise behind the 1967 edition has not changed. The original preface called Golding an anomaly, a fact that was confirmed when he won the Nobel Prize in 1983. Critics were at a loss to find someone with whom he could be compared. There were, of course, the Greeks for the early novels; but for the later ones, it was difficult to find analogues. Golding's themes are so archetypal that his fiction tends to recall a variety of works on similar subjects; the voyage in *Rites of Passage* brings to mind *Moby-Dick* and *Billy Budd*, but neither is really appropriate. Therefore, comparisons have been made either with works that have clearly influenced Golding or with those that are so close thematically that comparisons are valid.

The revised edition ends with a discussion of Golding's Nobel Prize, one of the causes célèbres of recent literary history. For the first time in its history, a member of the Swedish Academy publicly dissented, claiming that Golding was unworthy of such international acclaim. His breach of etiquette prompted the academy to admit that Golding had been under consideration for three years! How Golding went from an obscure Wiltshire schoolmaster in 1954 to a major novelist ten years later; how he then fell into neglect for more than a decade, emerging at the end of the 1970s and becoming a Nobel laureate in the early 1980s is a fascinating tale in itself. The vicissitudes of Golding's literary career prove the need for continual reexamination of contemporary authors.

Bernard F. Dick

Fairleigh Dickinson University

Chronology

1911   19 September, William Golding born in Cornwall, England, to Alec Golding, Senior Assistant Master of Marlborough Grammar School, and Mildred Golding, an active worker for women's suffrage.

1930   Enters Brasenose College, Oxford, to read science before switching to literature.

1934   *Poems,* his first published work.

1935   Bachelor of Arts (Oxon).

1935–1939   "Wasted the next four years" (by his own admission) acting at Hampstead Everyman Theatre and Citizen House in Bath and then at a small non–West End London theater.

1939   Marries Ann Brookfield and accepts position teaching English and philosophy at Bishop Wordsworth's School in Salisbury.

1940   Enlists the Royal Navy where he spends the next five years.

1945   Returns to Bishop Wordsworth's School.

1954   *Lord of the Flies;* published in America the following year.

1955   *The Inheritors;* published in America in 1962. Fellow of the Royal Society of Literature.

1956   *Pincher Martin;* published in America as *The Two Deaths of Christopher Martin* in 1957.

1958   *The Brass Butterfly,* a play, first performed at Oxford under the direction of Alastair Sim, who played the Emperor in this and in the London production.

1959   *Free Fall.* American edition the following year.

1960–1962   Book reviewer for the *Spectator.*

1961   Master of Arts (Oxon); leaves teaching to devote full time to writing.

1961–1962   Writer-in-residence, Hollins College, Virginia; American college lecture tour.

1964   *The Spire.*

1966   Honorary Fellow, Brasenose College, Oxford; *The Hot Gates.*

1967   *The Pyramid.*

1970   Honorary Doctor of Letters, Sussex University.

1971   *The Scorpion God.*

1979   *Darkness Visible.*

1980   *Rites of Passage;* wins Booker-McConnell prize for best novel of 1980.

1982   *A Moving Target.*

1983   Nobel Prize for literature.

1984   *The Paper Men.*

1985   *An Egyptian Journal.*

Chapter One
The Thorns of Life
From Poetry to Prose

The perverseness of memory and the shortage of suitable dissertation topics will never allow an author's juvenilia to go unnoticed. Until his death, William Faulkner lived under the shadow of his early poetry. When students at the University of Virginia confronted him with it, he became apologetic, calling his poems youthful works and adding that once he realized his limitations as a poet, he turned to prose, "the next best thing."[1]

Poetry was William Golding's first love also, yet he too is uncomfortable about this aspect of his past. He dismisses his poetry with an upward turn of the wrist that disclaims all responsibility for it. "You might say I write prose because I can't write poetry," he confides, but with a nostalgic quiver in his voice.[2]

Yet Golding could—and did—write poetry; even when he turned to prose, it was to prose-poetry, as Faulkner did. The medium was unimportant; Golding was destined to be a writer who would use language so creatively that he would receive a Nobel Prize. As a child, he loved class recitation, reveling in standing up and delivering pieces he had learned by heart. Actually, he did more that recite: he listened to his peers, absorbing not only the content of their poems but also the rhythm.[3] When he was not listening and learning, he was pursuing his lifelong interest in language. At seven, he copied out word lists when he should have been doing his arithmetic. Soon he discovered Tennyson, who was "wholly accessible," but not to his father.

Alec Golding was a man of formidable intelligence: his son once said, "I have never met anybody who could do so much, was interested in so much, and who knew so much."[4] A Senior Assistant Master at the Marlborough Grammar School, which Golding himself attended, Alec had written textbooks on chemistry, botany, zoology, physics, and geography. He was also an accomplished musician, as his son was later, equally at home with the violin, cello, viola, piano, and flute. Alec decided his son should be a scientist. Believing that the ladder of learning culminated in the sciences, William Golding mastered Latin so he could enter Oxford. Once there, he found himself trapped in a curriculum at variance with his true interests. For two years (1930–32) he endured labs and lectures while looking for any diversion that would take him away from the dissecting table. He even submitted to hypnosis, although he proved too introspective for it.

Fortunately, Golding had classmates who understood him. One loaned him a typewriter on which he composed poetic reflections on nature, unrequited love, the call of the sea, and the seductions of rationalism. Another made a selection of the poems and sent it to Macmillan without Golding's knowledge. To his surprise, Golding received a check for five pounds. *Poems,* his first published work, appeared in 1934 as part of Macmillan's Contemporary Poets, a series that also included Yvonne ffrench, Hugh Macdiarmid, T.W. Ramsey, R.C. Trevelyan, and Norman C. Yendell. In 1934 *Poems* cost a shilling; in 1981, when the poet was known as the author of *Lord of the Flies,* the asking price was four thousand dollars.

Inevitably, *Poems* has attracted critics.[5] One should remember, however, that these "sub-Thomas, sub-Keats" creations, as Golding dubbed them, were undergraduate productions, no better and no worse than the annual heartburst of the sensitive English major. As literature, they have no great value; but as documents illustrating the young Golding's concerns, they indicate that he was preoccupied with two themes that later became dominant motifs in his fiction: the divided society and single-minded rationalism.

In a sonnet entitled "Non-Philosopher's Song" he makes a distinction between heart and head: "Love and Reason live apart / In separate cells of head and heart." The novels also depict a dichotomy between two worlds and a polarization of two wisdoms. But in the sonnet, the poet's lady, like the Dantean *donna,* links the two worlds: "But oh! my lady, she and I, / We give philosophy the lie." To the young Golding, love is a bridge; it conquers and, in fact, bridges all. But later Golding, who graduated from Oxford as the world was moving toward a war in which he would soon be involved, could not recapture the optimism of his college days. "There is no bridge," declares Sammy Mountjoy, Golding's persona, in *Free Fall.*

Golding always objected to a catechetical view of the universe and to a reduction of human behavior to equations. The rationalist, a familiar Golding character whose mind has developed at the expense of his emotions, assumes various guises—Piggy in *Lord of the Flies,* Nick Shales in *Free Fall,* Phanocles in *The Brass Butterfly,* Talbot in *Rites of Passage.* But he is always the oversimplifier trying to tidy up a human heart that is often in disarray, or else he is the pragmatist who sees only surfaces and never the dark recesses that cry for illumination.

Even in his youth Golding was an antirationalist; his poem "Mr. Pope," the most significant in the collection, is an attack on devotion to a rationally conceived ideal with the neoclassical poet as target. What is refreshing about the poem is the wit that informs it, which keeps satire from degenerating into invective:

> Mr. Pope walked in the park—
> Trim rows of flowers
> Embroider'd the well-order'd dark
> Where marched the marshalled hours.
>
> The trees stood silent, two by two
> Pagodas lifted up their heads
> From neatly weeded laurel-groves
> And well-spaced flower-beds.
>
> Then down a quiet gravel path—
> For Mr. Pope eschewed the sod—
> The gentleman pursued his way
> To raise his hat to Mr. God.
>
> "Dear Sir," he said, "I must confess
> This is a chastely ordered land,
> But one thing mars its loveliness,
> The stars are rather out of hand"—
>
> "If they would dance a minuet
> Instead of roaming wild and free
> Or stand in rows all trim and neat
> How exquisite the sky would be!"

Golding never lost his suspicion of a discipline that only develops one aspect of the self, whether it is neoclassicism or a science that shuns the eternal for the temporal. He always chided "those who think they have an easy answer to all problems simply because they have never looked further than the rash appearing on the skin."[6]

To the Wars and Back

Twenty years elapsed before Golding published again, but he was by no means idle during those decades. First, he was engaged in World War II, which completely shattered his Candide-like optimism: "When I was young, before the war, I did have some airy-fairy views about man. . . . But I went through the war and that changed me. The war taught me different and a lot of others like me."[7] Second, Golding turned to Greek literature "not because it was the snobbish thing to do or even the most enjoyable, but because this is where the meat is."[8] It was while reading Greek and teaching at Bishop Wordsworth's School in Salisbury that Golding decided he wanted to become a novelist. His first four novels never saw publication and are not extant. Golding also claims to have written literary parodies for his own amusement during this period. These are equally as tantalizing a loss to the modern critic as the novels.

Significantly, his first published novel, *Lord of the Flies*, is a kind of parody, but not in the sense of a lampoon or a travesty, since Golding does not attach anything pejorative to the word. To him, parody "is subtly rooted in admiration."[9] His concept is very close to T. S. Eliot's notion of "mature" borrowing—transforming the work of one's predecessors into something that is at once traditional and novel. If it is to be successful, however, parody must also be critical. At the 1963 meeting of the American Philological Association, L. A. MacKay in his paper "Hero and Theme in the *Aeneid*" called Virgil's epic a "serious parody" of Homer, not in the sense that Virgil's intention was to subvert the *Iliad* and the *Odyssey,* but rather to transform them into something meaningful to his age. Death, for example, is a common occurrence in Homer, and the battle scenes in the *Iliad* are often merely gruesome and devoid of human significance. Virgil, however, uses Homer's battle descriptions in order to transform them into an indictment of war itself. This was Virgil's way of saying that, to a "modern" of the first century B.C., war is more than a series of conventional descriptions or epic formulae.

As a result of his classical reading, Golding was steeped in a literature in which originality consisted of uniting "tradition and the individual talent." His first novel is, in many respects, an outgrowth of his literary heritage—a parody in his own sense of the term. Thus there is nothing startlingly original about the "marooned boys" theme of *Lord of the Flies*; the same situation is found in "survival literature" and even in science fiction. If one feels the spirit of the Greeks hovering over *Lord of the Flies,* Golding would concur: "If I really had to adopt literary parentage. . . . I should name thunderous great names like Euripides, and Sophocles, and perhaps even Herodotus. And I might go so far as to say that I have a profound admiration. . . . for Homer."[10] *Lord of the Flies* is really a reworking of a boyhood favorite, Robert Michael Ballantyne's *Coral Island,* by a man who saw his youthful illusions shattered by a world war and then withdrew into Greek literature, "where the meat is."

Chapter Two

The Anarchy Within

Barefoot Boys

In 1857 Ballantyne published *The Coral Island,* something of a children's classic in England, in which three boys are shipwrecked on an unidentified Pacific island—Ralph Rover, the fifteen-year-old narrator; Jack Martin, "a tall, strapping broad-shouldered youth of eighteen, with a handsome, good-humoured, firm face"; and Peterkin Gay, "little, quick, funny, decidedly mischievous, and about fourteen years old."[1] The lads live in "uninterrupted harmony and happiness," presumably without the aftereffects of original sin, although faint, post-lapsarian rumblings can be heard in some of their activities, especially in Peterkin's butchery of an old sow to get leather for "future" shoes. These intimations of mortality are muted, however, since Victorian schoolboys do not kill for pleasure. Cannibals are also encountered, but heathen bloodletting can be overlooked. At the end of the novel, just as the boys think they will be devoured by savages, they are released into the hands of their deus-ex-machina teacher who announces that "through the great goodness of God you are free!" (310). The natives embrace Christianity, and all is well.

To a generation that has witnessed two world wars, Ballantyne's resolution is laughable. One is tempted to repeat Judge Brack's feeble reaction to Hedda Gabbler's suicide, "People don't do things like that," and to consign *The Coral Island* to the bedtime reading of the very young, the very old, or historians of ideas.

Golding clearly intended *Lord of the Flies* (1954) as a realist's answer to *The Coral Island:* "You see, really, I'm getting at myself in this [novel]. What I'm saying to myself is, 'Don't be such a fool, you remember when you were a boy, a small boy, how you lived on that island with Ralph and Jack and Peterkin. . . . Now you are grown up, you are adult; it's taken you a long time to become adult, but now you've got there you can see that people are not like that; they would not behave like that if . . . they went to an island like that."[2]

Golding's protagonists are also named Ralph and Jack; Peterkin be-

6

comes the overweight Piggy. Simon is an independent creation, although Golding for some unknown reason has claimed that Simon was inspired by Peterkin, perhaps meaning that the name of Peterkin evoked that of Simon Peter of the New Testament—two names deriving from one. Along with an indeterminate number of other boys ranging in age from six to twelve, they are abandoned on a South Sea island after being evacuated from Britain during a nuclear war. Like the Ballantyne trio, they also hunt pigs; but none of the Victorian boys would ever have sodomized the animal with a spear, since sexual defilement is apparently a vice peculiar to the post-Ballantyne age. Moreover, there is no "uninterrupted harmony and happiness" on Golding's coral island; the rules that Ralph thought would transform the motley group into a model utopia are irrevocably broken when the desire to hunt supersedes the need for a continually burning fire, shelter, and sanitation. The hunters don war paint, killing or absorbing all the others except Ralph who, in his refusal to revert to savagery, becomes a pariah, and is hunted down and smoked out of hiding. Fortunately, a navy cruiser spots the smoke, and Ralph and the remnants of the group are rescued after their initiation into adulthood.

Lord of the Flies introduces a structural principle that has become Golding's hallmark—a polarity expressed in terms of a moral tension: the rational (fire-watchers) pitted against the irrational (hunters) in *Lord of the Flies*; one species destroyed and supplanted by another that is supposedly fitter (*The Inheritors*); fallen humanity defying God (*Pincher Martin*); science at odds with humanism (*Free Fall*); the vision versus the reality (*The Spire*); the mystic juxtaposed with the nihilist (*Darkness Visible*); the classical sensibility giving way to the romantic (*Rites of Passage*); the creative writer pursued by the academic hack (*The Paper Men*).

Although the polarity is moral, the resolution is literary. Golding expresses his moral vision through traditional literary themes (odyssey, quest, journey to self-knowledge) and characters (castaways, overreachers, repressed clergymen, writer-celebrities), incorporating them into a narrative that ends conventionally (rescue, fulfillment, death, *anagnorisis*), if disturbingly. In *Lord of the Flies* Golding starts from what might be called the "island premise." All island literature is essentially similar in the sense that castaways can live either in harmony or anarchy. And like all drama, island literature is potentially tragic or comic, depending upon the author's vision. The "abandoned child" theme can produce Sophocles' *Oedipus the King* or Oscar Wilde's *Importance of*

Being Earnest; the theme of the individual challenging authority can result in Sophocles' *Antigone* or Garson Kanin's *Born Yesterday*; each, whether tragedy or comedy, is a valid elaboration of an archetypal situation. Since there is tragic potential in the comic, and seeds of comedy in the tragic, it is the author who determines the outcome. Ballantyne chose order; Golding chaos.

Island literature usually depicts three types of characters—children (*The Coral Island*), adults (*Robinson Crusoe*), or a combination (*The Swiss Family Robinson*). Following his source, Golding adheres to the first. As a novelist, he must offer some explanation for the absence of adults: "He [the pilot] must have flown off after he dropped us."[3] Thus far there is nothing unique about the situation except for the peculiarly modern use of a nuclear war to account for the evacuation.

The next events follow directly from the island premise. Piggy discovers a seashell ("the conch"), which Ralph uses as a trumpet to summon the others who are dispersed throughout the island. Last to appear is "something dark"; the amorphous blackness becomes an "it," then a "creature," and finally a party of boys—Jack Merridew and his choir. Jack immediately reveals his impatience with talk, asserting his claim to be chief because he was chapter chorister. It is Ralph, however, who wins, and the society splits into two halves: the fire-watchers and the choir turned hunters. From this point on, the plot can take only one course. Golding has imposed his own template on *The Coral Island,* and the lines zigzag, refusing to coincide with Ballantyne's.

The factionalized society in *Lord of the Flies* is not so much a case of antithesis as of polarization. Ralph seems to be the hero, although a close reading can prove otherwise. At the beginning, however, he has heroic potential. Ralph is fair-haired, with "a mildness . . . that proclaimed no devil." Jack, on the other hand, is satanic; his hair is red (a color often associated with Old Nick), he is dressed in black, and his eyes stare ahead. Furthermore, he is ugly and prone to anger. Jack is hardly the "handsome, good-humoured" lad he was in his Victorian incarnation.

An unspoken animosity stemming from their opposite natures arises between the two boys; it manifests itself in impatience, angry outbursts followed by sullen silence, and occasional attempts at coalescence. But these are only temporary solutions to an antagonism so ancient that neither Ralph nor Jack can fathom it. Later, Ralph asks the inevitable question "Why do you hate me?" There is no answer; there can be none with adolescents who do not realize they are embodiments of forces they do not understand, much less can name. Having read neither the Greeks nor Nietzsche, they do not know they are the embodiments of the Apollonian and the Dionysian, respectively.

Two Worlds, Two Wisdoms

During his self-imposed exile from contemporary life, Golding immersed himself in Greek literature, devoting a considerable amount of time to studying E. R. Dodds's edition of Euripides' *Bacchae*.[4] The *Bacchae* is a landmark of Greek tragedy; to paraphrase Pope, to know the *Bacchae* is to know the Greeks; and to know it in Dodds's edition with its detailed introduction and exhaustive notes is to know it as thoroughly as any contemporary can.

The *Bacchae,* probably Euripides' last play and the most complex of the Greek tragedies, dramatizes the impact of the worship of Dionysus on the city of Thebes. To the ancient Greeks, Dionysus was the god of animal potency, the mythological incarnation of the life principle; it was Dionysus who gave life to plant, animal, and human. He could inspire his votaries to frenzy, perhaps even to human sacrifice. Dionysus symbolizes the elemental in animal and human nature; as such, he cannot be ignored, for to inhibit emotional expression is to deny humankind a natural form of worship. Dionysus can be gentle when he is propitiated, but when he is rejected, he exacts a terrible vengeance. His opposite is Apollo, who personifies the civilizing arts—healing, poetry, music, law, and order. Identified with light, he illuminates rather than beclouds the mind.

In *The Birth of Tragedy out of the Spirit of Music,* Friedrich Nietzsche made his famous distinction between the Apollonian and the Dionysian, attributing all art to the tension and interplay between these forces. Initially, Apollo and Dionysus are at odds with each other; Apollo represents the god in humankind, Dionysus the brute. Apollo favors the individual; Dionysus appeals to the group. Apollo invites us to enter a dream world, like Homer's Olympus, where we can find refuge from reality. Dionysus, on the other hand, pulls away the veil of illusion, revealing the world as it is in all its savagery. Ultimately, the Apollonian manages to master the Dionysian so that art is able to assume some form and order; yet at the center of all great art is Dionysian wisdom, knowledge bred of suffering. At the beginning of *The Birth of Tragedy,* Nietzsche tries to be impartial, yet it is obvious that he favors the Dionysian; without the Dionysian, real art, tragic art (to

Nietzsche, the highest form) is impossible. While no art form is exclusively Apollonian or Dionysian, Nietzsche considers some predominately Apollonian (epic, painting, sculpture, pre-Wagnerian opera) and others largely Dionysian (music, lyric poetry, tragedy, Wagnerian opera). He concedes that in tragedy Apollo provides the form, but it is Dionysus who provides the content.

Lord of the Flies can be read in the light of the Apollonian-Dionysian dichotomy. In fact, this interpretation has been standard ever since Golding declared his debt to Greek tragedy, especially to the *Bacchae*, in which Euripides immortalized the age-old conflict between mind and heart, reason and emotion, showing that the way up and down is not the same, as Heraclitus believed, but rather that both paths must continually cross without superseding each other.[5] In the *Bacchae*, Pentheus, king of Thebes, is rooted in a frigid intellectualism that does not allow for the irrational. When the worship of Dionysus sweeps through the country, claiming Pentheus's mother, Agave, and the high priest Teiresias as followers (not to mention Cadmus, the city's founder), Pentheus is still unyielding; he refuses to acknowledge the new religion, even though Cadmus and Teiresias caution him that he must at least give it a hearing. Dionysus himself warns Pentheus; in a startling scene the god appears before him as a bull, one of the animal forms in which Dionysus was worshiped. Pentheus can only gape at the metamorphosis, unaware that he is in the presence of the god he is persecuting. When Dionysus induces Pentheus to observe the Bacchants at worship, he suggests that Pentheus wear women's clothes to escape detection. It is a logical suggestion; Dionysus's chief votaries are women, and male worshipers are expected to wear the fawnskin and carry the ivy-garlanded *thyrsus*. At the height of the ritual, Dionysus reveals the presence of Pentheus, who is observing from high up in a fir tree. Goaded by a frenzy that makes them oblivious to moral laws, the women hunt him down and dismember him. Triumphant, Agave, still under the Dionysian influence and thinking that she holds the head of a lion (another of Dionysus's sacred animals), appears with her son's head on a *thyrsus*. Although there is a break in the text at verse 1329, it is clear from the plot summary attached to certain manuscripts and from the final scene, that Dionysus appeared at the end of the play and banished Agave from her native Thebes.

Both *Lord of the Flies* and the *Bacchae* portray a bipolar society in which the Apollonian refuses or is unable to assimilate the Dionysian. Just as Pentheus's refusal to admit Dionysian worship polarizes Thebes,

Ralph's inability to understand the hunters, whose Dionysian character is underscored by their being black-clad choristers, polarizes the island. Both drama and novel contain three interrelated ritual themes: the cult of a beast-god, a hunt as prefiguration of the death of a scapegoat-figure, and the dismemberment of the scapegoat. Golding deviates from Euripides in only one respect. Logically, Ralph, the Pentheus figure, should be the scapegoat; but Golding assigns this role to Simon, one of the choristers, who has clairvoyant powers. Ralph is allowed to live with his newfound knowledge of "the darkness of man's heart." Otherwise Golding has adhered to the ritual pattern of *agon* or struggle between king and rival (Pentheus and Dionysus, Ralph and Jack), *pathos* or suffering (Pentheus, Ralph), and *sparagmos* or dismemberment (Pentheus, Simon, replacing Ralph, as scapegoat).

The Boy Bacchants

Euripides depicts a Dionysus who retains the original characteristics of a beast deity incarnate in the form of bulls, lions, wild goats, and fawns. Since these animals were regarded as habitations of the god, they were often torn apart by the Bacchants, who would eat their flesh to achieve communion with Dionysus. As human and animal, Dionysus is both hunter and hunted. Thus beast-hunt imagery pervades the *Bacchae* (verses 101, 137, 436, 920, 1017, 1188 ff.). In *Lord of the Flies* the obsession with the hunt transforms the hunters into a group that functions conjointly but without personal identity; they had "the throb and stamp of a single organism." Their choral refrain "*Kill the beast! Cut his throat! Spill his blood!*" suggests the "hunt, kill, prey" of the *Bacchae*. In the drama, Pentheus's death is prefigured by the Bacchants' attack on a herd of cattle that they dismember. In *Lord of the Flies* the wanton killing of a sow prefigures the death of Simon. The sow's head is impaled on a stick (a reminiscence of Pentheus's head on the *thyrsus*) and is offered as a trophy to the imaginary beast the boys believe is lurking on the island. When Simon accidentally interrupts the reenactment of the pig hunt, he is mistaken for the beast and killed; when the Bacchants spot Pentheus in the fir tree, they drag him down under the delusion that he is the beast and then dismember him.

Both Pentheus and Simon are pitted against elemental forces that are their direct opposites. Pentheus alone sees Dionysus in animal shape, but he can neither recognize the god nor understand that his own intellectualism must be complemented by irrational yet necessary passions. Only Simon hears the cynical message of the "Lord of the Flies," the spirit of evil personified by the pig's head, assuring Simon that "everything was a bad business." Although Simon is an epileptic whom even Ralph considers "cracked" and whose seizures annoy Jack, he could have explained to the group—had he lived—about a natural proclivity to evil that can subvert harmony and order. Pentheus dies ignorant of his nature and that of humankind; Simon dies with a knowledge that he can never articulate.

Another point of similarity between Euripides and Golding is the deus-ex-machina ending of both works. At the end of the *Bacchae,* Dionysus appears to foretell the fortunes of all. A more human epiphany occurs at the end of the novel when a naval officer comes to the rescue, thereby resolving the action. In view of the previous bloodshed, however, Golding's ending is as ironic as Euripides'; it is also less obvious. Euripides' ending is a deus ex machina in the literal sense of the god's descending from a crane, but not in the conventional sense of outside intervention in order to resolve the plot. In the *Poetics,* Aristotle allowed for such an ending if the action could not be resolved in any other way. The *Bacchae,* however, does not involve outside intervention because Dionysus is not outside the action; he is very much a part of it. In fact, he is a character in his own play. The naval officer is external to the action; he is a deus ex machina like Heracles in Sophocles' *Philoctetes* or Apollo in Euripides' *Orestes,* neither of whom appears until the end.

In *Philoctetes* and *Orestes,* mortals have allowed the action to get so out of hand that divine intervention is necessary. But so have the boys in *Lord of the Flies*; hence the "god from the machine." Although Golding called his own ending a "gimmick,"[6] thus introducing a word that would plague him, his "gimmick" is certainly as legitimate as the one in Bertolt Brecht's *Three Penny Opera,* in which the Victorious Messenger arrives just in time to save Macheath from the gallows, although in Brecht's play the audience is warned that real-life messengers are rare.

Like Brecht, Golding has a reason for using an ex-machina ending. First, he wishes to parody Ballantyne's ending of *The Coral Island,* which is true gimmickry; second, he wishes to capture the uneasiness the Greeks must have felt in watching the *Bacchae* when that play, which was unfolding logically, suddenly took its irrational turn. Readers disturbed by Golding's ending might find comfort in knowing that the Greeks found Euripides' sense of denouement equally discomfiting:

"I have always felt that the Athenians must have been deeply shocked by the *deus ex machina*. Here they had been watching a play with a beginning, a middle, and instead of an ending, one has a god coming down resolving everything."[7]

A Dionysian Is Made As Well As Born

Among the many instances of Golding's debt to Euripides is his reproduction of the Dionysian-Apollonian *agon* which, like that in the *Bacchae*, is depicted as a clash not so much of wills as of extremes. The *Bacchae* is an account of a Dionysian worship whose excesses are seen not as the result of ecstasy or orgiastic ritual but as a reaction to Apollonian intolerance. In the prologue, Dionysus makes it clear that he is punishing Thebes for growing so enlightened (no doubt because of Pentheus's rationalism) that it has denied his divinity by refusing to recognize his mother, Semele, as Zeus's consort. To vindicate his godhead as well as his mother's honor, Dionysus adopts a course of action—mass conversion—that will leave no doubt as to his parentage.

Although Dionysus is an alien god whose worship began in Asia Minor before spreading to Greece, he insists on his due. So does Jack Merridew in *Lord of the Flies*, and precisely because he comes from an alien tradition. What sets Jack apart from the others is his educational background: Jack comes from a cathedral school where he was a prefect and probably a scholarship student, which his being chapter chorister seems to suggest. Just as the Bacchants had their distinctive attire (fawnskin, *thyrsus*), Jack and his choristers wear black caps with silver badges and black cloaks emblazoned with silver crosses. Since Jack considers himself unique, he demands to be chief, claiming among his other attributes that he can sing C-sharp. Thus he appears to be a true son of Dionysus, who favored song over speech. Unlike the others who use first names, Jack introduces himself by his last name, thus disassociating himself from Apollonian individuation in favor of Dionysian group identity.

Like Euripides, Golding implies that a moderate Dionysianism can be beneficial to society while an immoderate Apollonianism can be fatal. Ralph is an incipient Pentheus, rational but immature. Pentheus ridicules Dionysus for his long hair, which he cuts to make the god conform to the Greek ideal of manhood. While Pentheus's immaturity is that a book-burner and witch-hunter, Ralph's is that of an adolescent. Ralph squeals with glee and turns somersaults; he calls his friend, whose real name he never attempts to learn, "Piggy," although he knows how much the boy hates it. Both Pentheus and Ralph are obsessed with what is "good"; Ralph applies the term to almost everything including the island ("it's a good island"). Since Ralph claims to possess "the good," he can legislate for those who lack it. While both Pentheus and Ralph claim to be natural rulers, neither offers much proof of leadership. Dionysus does all but admit who he is to Pentheus, even causing an earthquake and staging a prison escape; still, Pentheus does not recognize him. Ralph thinks he is on an island; Piggy knows he is on one. Ralph has no idea what the conch is; he thinks it is a stone. Piggy corrects him and shows him how to use it. Had Piggy been slimmer and not afflicted with asthma and myopia, he might have been elected chief.

Initially, Jack seems far more qualified to govern than Ralph. First, he is more logical. He does not "think" he is on an island; he tries to determine whether the place on which he has landed is completely surrounded by water. When Ralph wonders if the tracks on the island were made by humans, Jack must tell him they were made by animals. Jack is just as concerned about being rescued as Ralph; he also agrees on the need for rules. When Ralph proposes they build a fire to attract any ships that might be in the vicinity, Jack shouts approval. Yet neither Ralph nor Jack knows how to make a fire; each is embarrassed at being unable to provide what the situation requires. At least Jack does not ask if anyone has a match, as Ralph does. Jack also knows how a fire can be started: by using Piggy's specs as a burning glass.

By having Jack discover how to create fire, Golding deepens the nature of the *agon*: it is not only a clash between the Apollonian and the Dionysian but between the true and the false Prometheus. Jack, not Ralph, is the real Prometheus, the true fire-bearer. The dark god becomes the culture hero. The mythic inversion is ingenious, especially if one remembers that "Prometheus" literally means "Forethought."

A similar inversion occurs in the case of Piggy's glasses. On one level, the glasses are a symbol of political insight. As an inadequate leader, Ralph depends on Piggy's judgment. Like the other relationships in the novel, theirs also is paradoxical. Ralph must "see" through eyes that themselves need corrective lenses. Although Piggy's vision is imperfect, even with glasses, it is all Ralph has. While the lenses remain intact, Ralph can at least go through the motions of statesmanship; but the smashing of one of the lenses diminishes Piggy's effectiveness, and the theft of the other by the hunters renders Piggy useless and Ralph helpless.

On another, equally complex level, the glasses are a means of creating fire to which Ralph assigns an Apollonian function: rescue/reason, in the sense that reason must prevail if rescue is to come. Jack takes a more pragmatic view of fire; while he is the first to agree that rules are necessary and is willing to have part of the choir act as fire-watchers, he also regards fire as a means of roasting meat. Ralph seems oblivious to the cooking properties of fire; he would have everyone eat fruit, with an occasional crab, even though fruit causes diarrhea. Yet even Ralph succumbs to the temptation: twice he eats the meat that the hunters have cooked. When Ralph castigates the others for defecting because they wanted meat, Jack must remind him that he has a bone in his hand. The Dionysian can be even more perceptive than the Apollonian.

In Golding's fiction, just when one meaning seems to have been established, another arises to compete with it; just as one paradox is resolved, another takes its place; just as the ultimate irony seems to have been reached, it is no longer ultimate. For example, if fire symbolizes civilization, as well as the means of returning to it, rescue is in vain because civilization is in the process of being destroyed. Moreover, fire may be an Apollonian symbol of rescue, but a Dionysian has made rescue possible by using fire to smoke Ralph out of hiding, thereby accomplishing what Ralph could not: to attract a passing ship. Perhaps the most ironic aspect of fire is that it is not a "small" Apollonian fire, the kind Piggy wanted, that effects the rescue; and it is not the fire on the mountain that Ralph wanted (and that, under the circumstances, would have been futile). It is a vast Dionysian fire, one that sets the jungle ablaze; only a fire raging out of control could generate enough smoke to attract attention.

Self-multiplying ambivalence is the way Golding has chosen to illustrate his theory of evil. Although evil is indigenous to the species and impervious even to the waters of baptism, it remains dormant until the right set of circumstances activates it. Just when one thinks reason will prevent evil from occurring, reason breaks down because those supposedly endowed with it either fail to exercise it or are not as rational as they seemed to be. Yet Golding is not really a fatalist, much less a Calvinist or an exponent of the Heidelberg Catechism. Fate and free will coexist in his universe. Evil is bound to erupt, but it requires,

like T. S. Eliot's objective correlative, an event or a situation to pre-
cipitate it; a situation that humans cause themselves and for which
there is a human explanation.

The crucial event in *Lord of the Flies* is not Jack's losing the election;
that would be too easy. Jack's defeat did not turn him from a potential
Apollonian into an incorrigible Dionysian. Jack lost the election because his manner alienated the others, who perceived him as a martinet
or as a prefect who might bully them as their prefects had in school.
They thought that Jack would also call them by their surnames as their
teachers did. Ralph is less threatening; he can sound like an adult yet
act like a child, insisting on rules as well as on having fun.

Interestingly, Jack is gracious in defeat; he is even cooperative. In a
rare moment of magnanimity, Ralph asks Jack what role he wants to
play in the newly formed society. Jack immediately chooses the role of
hunter for himself and the choir; it is a wise decision since the boys
need something to eat besides fruit. Jack sees an opportunity for himself and his choir to perform a meaningful function: they will kill pigs
and provide the community with meat. What Jack does not know,
however, is that Ralph regards the hunter as an inferior. Although
Ralph has given Jack his choice of role, he determines how Jack will
play it. By downgrading the hunter, Ralph exalts himself, thereby
becoming a Pentheus and forcing the choir to become Dionysians.

Learning the Part

Becoming a Dionysian is a gradual process. There are times when
the Dionysian seems so accommodating that coalescence appears possible. Ralph and Jack smile at each other when Ralph asks Jack his
preference; they smile at each other again while gathering wood. But
smiles are deceptive as well as evanescent. Ralph smiles at Simon when
the latter predicts his rescue, but it is the smile of one whose spirits
have been elevated. That the one who elevated them is "cracked" is
irrelevant. There are also moments when some of the Dionysian rubs
off on the Apollonian. After his encounter with a charging boar, Ralph
participates in the reenactment of the incident, becoming so caught up
in the drama that "the desire to squeeze and hurt was over-mastering"
(142). Jack and Ralph are doubles, a favorite Golding device in which
one character is the reverse of the other and the extreme opposite in
terms of qualities. What they have in common is a plan for survival
and an ability to take control of a situation, although in both respects

Jack has an edge on Ralph. What causes the rift between them, and what widens the rift into an abyss, is Ralph's monolithic view of fire, which adumbrates his relationship with Jack. By limiting the function of fire to rescue and by regarding it as a panacea, Ralph excludes all other possibilities for its use. When Jack tries to tell Ralph about the dark urges he experiences while hunting, Ralph admonishes him not to forget the fire; "You and your fire!" is Jack's frustrated retort.

Gradually, ineluctably, Ralph is turning Jack into a Dionysian. Although Jack chooses the role of hunter, Ralph makes him live the part, not realizing that the myth requires the hunter also to be the hunted; just as the hunter stalks his prey, Dionysus stalks the hunter. Jack tries to explain this paradox to Ralph, who is too preoccupied with the fire to care: "'If you're hunting sometimes you catch yourself feeling as if—' He [Jack] flushed suddenly. 'There's nothing in it of course. Just a feeling. But you can feel as if you're not hunting, but—being hunted; as if something's behind you all the time in the jungle. . . . Ralph looked at him critically through his tangle of fair hair. 'So long as you and your hunters remember the fire—'" (67–68).

The hunter is a role Jack can play, although he must grow into it; he is not typecast. The first time Jack sees a pig, he is unable to kill it. Since Ralph is both director and writer of his utopian scenario, he criticizes Jack's performance: "You should stick a pig. . . . They always talk about sticking a pig." As the son of a naval commander, Ralph apparently heard about pig-sticking in colonial India. Pig-sticking was the equivalent of bear-baiting, if one is to believe Noel Coward, who, in one of his songs, told of the Briton who "took to pig-sticking / in quite the wrong way." Barry England dramatized the wrong way in his drama *Conduct Unbecoming,* in which a group of officers, for whom pig-sticking was subliminated sodomy, attempted the same with a woman.

A pig is slain in *Lord of the Flies*; it is also sodomized with a pointed stick. Again, and this is something that can only be appreciated in retrospect, Golding is implying that anyone can take to pig-sticking in the wrong way. Even the British empire has its dark side, which is suddenly, and tragically, illuminated when one of the boys calls for the sow's degradation: "Right up her ass!" (168).

As repellent as the incident is, it is still a scene in a drama that originated with Ralph, except now the plot has gotten out of hand. None of the boys is a natural pig-sticker any more than a natural murderer. If there is a defect in the species, in the fullness of time and under the proper circumstances, it will be revealed. Golding is quite clear on this point; he is not caught on the horns of the nature-versus-nurture dilemma, because he believes that nature is defective, and therefore everything associated with it, including its institutions, is defective also. Within the child are the seeds of evil that will eventually flower.

In *Lord of the Flies,* however, it is a child who waters the dark bloom and brings another's evil to blossom. Although Jack chose the role of hunter, Ralph specifies how he will play it: as Dionysian hunter. That particular role is foreign to Jack; he must rehearse it. Jack goes down on all fours, "his nose only a few inches from the humid earth" (61). He practices crouching, slithering, crawling; yet still he has not learned the part. What forces him to master the role and then play it to the hilt is Ralph's refusal to forgive him and the hunters for letting the fire go out. Ralph, on the other hand, cannot master his role because it is beyond his capabilities; he might be the president of a school club but not the governor of an island. Ralph could possibly command a ship, like his father; but an island is not a ship, only a microcosmic ship of state, of which Ralph proves a poor captain.

Ralph also does not seem to like his role. In a telling moment, when both boys are on the verge of speaking openly, Ralph blurts out: "You want to hunt! While I—" (69). Ralph is insecure in his part, and the reason, Golding intimates, is that he is neither qualified for, nor suited to, it. It is also a role for which his class has not prepared him.

Class Consciousness on Coral Island

Golding has often remarked that, among other things, *Lord of the Flies* is about British society and particularly about class structure.[8] Like other interpretations, this one must be extricated from a narrative that has been skillfully woven. Although Golding tells the reader virtually nothing about most of the boys, he does provide—comparatively, at least—a good deal of background information about Ralph. We know, for instance, that he was a naval officer's son; Jack's parentage, on the other hand, is unknown. In a significant and usually ignored episode in chapter 7, Ralph dreams about the Dartmoor cottage where he lived with his parents. The cottage is especially meaningful to him because it was his last real home, after which his father's reassignments resulted in continual relocation. Even at twelve, Ralph can recall "a succession of homes." The Dartmoor cottage is doubly significant because "mummy had still been with them and Daddy had come home every day." Clearly, after Ralph had been packed off to school, Mummy was no longer with them, and Daddy did not come home every day since there was apparently no home to come to. Constant uprooting produced in Ralph a desire for stability and a need to stay in one place; hence he restricts the boys to the shore. His father instilled in him a sense of regimentation and a respect for order; hence he insists not on rules but on "more rules." More than what, one might ask, since Ralph has not yet formulated any rules. Ralph thinks in terms of excess: not rules, but more rules because one cannot get enough of them. His vaulting Apollonianism is even more evident when he calls for "more wood" for the fire which then proceeds to burn out of control. Ideally, Ralph should be a skipper where his sphere of influence would be limited to the confines of the vessel, and his penchant for assigning tasks and restricting activity might pass for maritime ability.

It is not coincidental that the island is boat-shaped: "it was roughly boat-shaped, humped near this end with behind them the humbled descent to the shore" (38). In a later and more intricate novel, *Rites of Passage,* Golding uses a ship, on which a white line separates the afterdeck from the quarterdeck, as a microcosm of British society. Even when he was writing *Lord of the Flies,* Golding was thinking of a ship as a metaphor of social stratification where the "class" in which one chooses to travel is dependent on one's social and economic background. Ralph behaves like a first-class passenger; because he feels superior to Piggy, whose parents are dead and whose aunt owns a candy store, he can order him about ("Get my clothes," he demands). Because Ralph attaches no importance to being a chorister or a prefect, he can be intolerant of Jack.

Ralph even extends his notions of class consciousness to the island which, topographically, lends itself to stratification. Ralph favors the shore; the hunters, the jungle. Once the boys discover that the peninsula is a natural fortress, they take possession of it and dub it Castle Rock. By the end of the novel, the entire island has been polarized, from the Apollonian shore to the Dionysian tip.

Although it may seem that Golding has grafted the class-consciousness theme onto the novel, it should be remembered that the same theme appeared in one of his sources. In the *Bacchae,* Euripides emphasizes that one of the most appealing features of Dionysian worship is its leveling of all distinctions. Dionysus is egalitarian; his appeal is to the masses. Apollo is elitist, and so is Ralph. Apollo was served by priests and priestesses. Similarly, Ralph requires a cabinet, yet it consists of one person—Piggy—whom he takes on as advisor. He ignores Jack who would have made a splendid defense minister. Simon could have been spiritual leader/high priest, but he is "batty" and "cracked." Furthermore, Simon cannot articulate his insights in the kind of direct speech Ralph requires.

Golding's island is a dystopia in which the classes do not cooperate for the common good. Instead of being chief of state, Ralph devolves into a minister of sanitation, preoccupied with shelter and exasperated by the boys' indifference to hygiene. Instead of being a defense minister, Jack reverts to a tribal warrior, emulating King Kong and Tarzan. Instead of being a peacemaker, Simon withdraws to a secluded part of the island inhabited by butterflies. It may be a fitting place for one so spiritual, since the Greek word for spirit, *psyche,* means both soul and butterfly. Ascetic withdrawal, however, accomplishes nothing when a world is in chaos. Yet this is Golding's point: evil is so endemic that its effects are everywhere, even in the actions of the good; we are on a good island, but it is an island where a leader cannot achieve the good by creating harmony among the classes. Thus Ralph, Piggy, Jack, and Simon go their own ways, along with what they symbolize. Piggy realizes Ralph's limitations as a leader and votes for him with reluctance. Piggy cannot function as a prime minister because he cannot help Ralph remove the one obstacle that stands in the way of unity: his antagonism toward Jack. But the main reason why Piggy cannot help Ralph is that Piggy himself is part of the problem. Jack loathes Piggy for his prissiness and for Ralph's reliance on him; from Jack's point of view, he is the one on whom Ralph should rely. Ideally, a dyarchy should have been established, but that would have been impossible since Ralph wanted to be chief. One would think Simon might have been able to help; as a chorister, he is part of Jack's world and should understand the sense of oneness that grows out of choral song. Simon, however, prefers solitude and Ralph's company to Jack's—understandably, since Jack has little patience with him and finds his fainting spells wearisome. There can therefore be no moral resolution, only a literary one—a deus ex machina; the situation has moved out of human bounds into the domain of the deity who alone can end the war between spirit and matter.

Beelzebub, Prince of Devils

Eventually, one must confront the meaning of the title which, like all of Golding's symbolism, derives from the narrative itself. "Lord of the Flies" is a translation of *Beelzebub,* the Greek transliteration of the Hebrew *Ba'alzevuv,* which in Judaism and Christianity denotes the principle of evil personified: the Devil, Satan, Mephistopheles. Golding equates the Lord of the Flies with the demonic force latent in humankind, a force so hideous, he notes, that fly-covered excrement would best represent it.

Evil is also an abstraction; it is a privation, the absence of the good. A novel, even an allegorical one, cannot portray abstraction. Thus Golding embodies evil in something concrete—in an animal's head swarming with flies. First the "littluns" insist a beast is lurking on the island. Ralph, Jack, and Simon consider their fears groundless, the product of their fitful imaginations. But when a dead paratrooper lands on the mountain top, bobbing up and down like a grotesque puppet, even Jack is forced to revise his opinion, thinking that the corpse is the beast, or rather a manifestation of the beast that, like Dionysus, can assume different forms. The boys can do nothing about the corpse-beast since they are afraid of approaching it; but they can try to appease it. Since they conceive of the beast as an animal, they make an animal offering to it; since pigs are plentiful on the island, their choice of offering has been made for them. This pig, however, is different from the first one that was slain: this pig is female. The attack has overtones of rape; the slaying culminates in defilement and decapitation.

In chapter 8, the hunters spot a sow and her young. The heat of the afternoon acts as an erotic stimulant; the animal's being female is an incentive for a rapelike assault; its being a mother is an invitation to perversity. The sow's screams intensify their desires the way the cries of a rape victim may excite a rapist instead of deterring him. The boys become "wedded to [the sow] in lust," with Jack becoming the chief bridegroom. While the others jab at the sow, Jack mounts her, "stabbing downward with his knife." Whether or not this is an oedipal wedding night, as one critic described it,[9] is debatable. It is, however, bestiality that stops short of intercourse—a stick driven into the sow's anus substituting for penetration. It is also scapegoating; an animal becomes an outlet for desires previously repressed but now unleashed upon a creature that cannot retaliate.

Dark of the Moon

As a classicist, Golding was familiar with Robert Graves's *White Goddess,* one of the most important studies of the mythmaking process ever written and one that is especially relevant to a discussion of *Lord of the Flies.* The White Goddess is the personification of the female in all her aspects, contradictory as they may be: maiden/crone, regenerator/destroyer, virgin/whore, human/animal. She was worshiped in a variety of forms, including the moon, and could even transform herself into animals such as the sow; hence the pig was sacred to the White Goddess. Understood as an avatar of the goddess, the sow in *Lord of the Flies* symbolizes both matriarchy and maternalism. Her presence has a negative effect on the boys who regard the sight of a mother with her young not as an image of domestic harmony but as a threat to their freedom. The sow suggests family, without which society, culture, and civilization are impossible. But family and all it represents is precisely what the boys have rejected, and anything that evokes the familial is repugnant to them, because they have chosen anarchy. They also associate family with Ralph, who tries to unite them, who imposes rules, and who preaches right and wrong. Ralph, then, is no different from the sow; everything he stands for—order, work, reprimands—has maternal overtones. Thus when the hunters declare Ralph an outlaw, Roger, Jack's sadistic lieutenant, sharpens a stick at both ends, planning to inflict the sow's fate on Ralph. And if the sow's death is paradigmatic, Ralph's death would also have included ritual sodomization as a fitting punishment for men who implement feminine values.

Since the stick had been sharpened at both ends, Ralph's head would have been impaled on one end like the sow's and offered to the beast. In the boys' Dionysian unconscious, the sow is both the beast (or a form of the beast) as well as an offering to the beast. Such duality, although it may seem contradictory, was consistent with the Dionysian religion in which both the god and his votaries were prey and predator, hunted and hunter. The Bacchants hunted Dionysus, who, in turn, hunted them. They hunted the god in his animal form; when they found his avatar, they often dismembered it and ate the raw flesh.

The slain animal was offered to Dionysus, as happens at the end of the *Bacchae* when Agave returns to Thebes, thinking she has killed a lion and planning to make a feast of its remains. Since gods die and are reborn, and since their animal forms are self-perpetuating, the paradox is resolvable: one can kill the god and then eat the god, thereby acquiring some of his power. The god lives on in his worshipers as well as in his animal incarnations. The pig in *Lord of the Flies* represents the same kind of Dionysian ambivalence: it is beast and beast-offering, sacramental meal and sacrificial victim.

That Golding intended the pig to be equated with the beast is evident from three incidents in the novel. First, there is the slaying of the sow and the impaling of its head, both of which are witnessed by Simon. When the hunters leave, Simon looks up at the head whose eyes assure him that "everything was a bad business" (170). Although the head has not spoken, Simon construes its look as an expression of despair in humanity; hence, his reply "I know that." Endowed with prophetic insight, he also knows the meaning of what he has seen: the beast and its offering are synonymous. While the Bacchants make the same connection, there is a major difference between their killing of the Dionysian animal and the hunters' killing of the sow. The Dionysian animal is not evil because what the animal represents—the god— is good. The sow, however, is evil because, to the hunters, everything she represents is evil. Although the sow's head is offered to the beast, it is still part of the beast; if the beast is evil, the head is the apotheosis of evil—the Lord of the Flies.

When the boys reenact the slaying, they chant: *"Kill the beast! Cut his throat! Spill his blood!"* (187). They think of the pig as related to the beast in some way, but are too immature to understand how complete the identification is. Yet neither the slaying nor its reenactment has produced the desired effect of emotional liberation. The Bacchants experience release because they feel no guilt in slaying the sacred animal. The hunters, however, feel guilt but repress it. They enjoy only a temporary cessation of fear; the orgasm of violence has not assuaged their anxieties. If it did, the beast would be dead or at least appeased, and Simon would not have been mistaken for it. By ritualizing the slaying, the boys are acting out of guilt and fear, like the brothers in Freud's *Totem and Taboo* who kill the primal father and, to salve their conscience, establish a yearly ritual commemorating his death.

The final association of pig with beast occurs when Simon journeys to the mountain and discovers that the arch-beast is really a dead paratrooper. The paratrooper's body is also covered with flies. Just as the boys projected evil into the sow, with the result that its head became the Lord of the Flies, so too have they demonized the paratrooper, who was as unthreatening as the sow. Evil, then, is born in fear and nurtured by guilt. It exists within us; when it is unleashed, it breeds like

flies, befouling whatever it alights on and swarming over what it has
befouled. Just as humankind creates its ogres, so have the boys who
made a pig's head emblematic of what was within them.

Evil is double-edged; it has a conscious and an unconscious dimension. History has made us conscious of its existence; yet evil can be
ahistorical, originating in the unconscious as fear of the unknown. Simon realizes that the beast reflects humankind's ambivalence toward
evil as a force both outside and within the self; he knows that the "beast
was harmless and horrible" (181). Yet these are also the characteristics
of irrational fear (harmless) and its effects (horrible). Simon senses that
this "news must reach the others as soon as possible." When he descends the mountain to bring the others the good news, he recalls
Moses coming down from Mount Sinai with the covenant. Moses found
the Israelites worshiping a golden calf; Simon finds the hunters reliving
the pig hunt. Simon becomes both the ritual intruder and the beast
because, in their perversion of the Dionysian ceremony, the boys cannot
make a distinction: each is evil, each must be destroyed. In the death
of Simon, Golding makes a subtle but important change in his retell-
ing of the *Bacchae*. While Pentheus was also intruder and beast, he was
not both simultaneously. First, he was the unholy witness to the rites;
later, in his mother's delirium, he was the beast of Dionysus. With a
cast of children, Golding cannot stage a mad scene as Euripides did for
Agave, nor can he have the boys come to a realization of what they
have done. That would defeat his purpose; the boys will never know
what they have done because, unlike the *Bacchae*, there is no god to
come down and tell them. Only Ralph knows, and he must live with
that knowledge for the rest of his life.

In the death of Simon, Golding has also made his definitive statement about the beast: the beast is *other*. Whatever one fears, whether
it is mythic like ogres and bogeymen, or real like countries and ideol-
ogies, it is not-I, beast, and ultimately evil. First, it was the pig; then
Simon; next Piggy; and if it were not for the Royal Navy, Ralph. All
the deaths occur because the victims are perceived as *other*; all the
deaths are variations on pig-slaying. Simon enters the hunters' circle
while they are chanting, *"Kill the beast! Cut his throat! Spill his blood!"*
Ralph was to suffer the sow's fate and by the same instrument. Piggy
not only dies with limbs twitching "like a pig's after it has been killed"
(223); Roger kills him the same way he speared the sow—by applying
leverage to a rock which comes crashing down on Piggy.

Simon alone receives a requiem from the author, which may suggest

Golding's fondness for his character or perhaps his fondness for *The White Goddess,* which helps to explain the novel's ambivalence. Both the fire-watchers and the hunters are, in some way, under the influence of the White Goddess: the hunters under her malefic form—Hecate, the moon in the underworld, the dark of the moon; the fire-watchers under her benign form—Diana, the moon goddess of the sky. When Simon is killed, the Moon officiates at his obsequies, wrapping him in a shroud of beams: "The line of his cheek silvered and the turn of his shoulder became sculptured marble" (190). That the most poetic part of *Lord of the Flies* follows a brutal murder is again evidence of Golding's debt to Graves, who also saw poetry coming out of ritual murder: "No poet can hope to understand the nature of poetry unless he has had a vision of the Naked King crucified to the lopped oak, and watched the dancers, red-eyed from the acrid smoke of the sacrificial fires, stamping out the measure of the dance, their bodies bent uncouthly forward, with a monotonous chant of: 'Kill! kill! kill!' and "Blood! blood! blood!'"[10]

The hunters' chant in *Lord of the Flies* is less monotonous, but the sentiments are the same; so is the source.

Flawed Classic or Classic Flaws?

Few first novels have been so powerfully conceived or so well written as *Lord of the Flies*; still, it is not without flaws. Its faults, however, are more attributable to the subject matter than to Golding's handling of it. Once Golding chose *The Coral Island* as his point of departure, he had no other choice but to use children as characters; once he merged *The Coral Island* with the *Bacchae,* he had no other choice but to make some of the children killers. Obviously, this was what Golding wanted. Children suited his moral purpose: as a potential adult, the child is as capable of anything—including evil—as the adult; if the child is shown to be naturally capable of evil, evil is endemic to the race.

Still, children have always posed a problem to the novelist, because they cannot disentangle cause and effect. The author must do it for them, explaining what would otherwise be dramatized or only inferable. In order to account for Simon's insight into the nature of evil, Golding makes him a visionary and a saint. Ballantyne did not have this problem since there was no Simon in *The Coral Island.* In creating Simon, Golding fell into a trap. Simon's realization of "mankind's essential illness" and his ability to visualize it as excrement are not characteristic of a child; nor are they necessarily characteristic of a saint. Traditionally, saints have been more attuned to God than to Satan; their knowledge of Satan was based on their knowledge of God: by understanding one, they understood the other. Simon, however, gives no evidence of understanding God, let alone His opposite.

At the end of the novel, Ralph weeps for "the darkness of man's heart." Yet Ralph is twelve, and what he knows about the darkness of the heart, despite what he has witnessed on the island, is minimal compared to what Anne Frank knew. In spite of everything, Anne believed people were essentially good. Ralph cannot even say they are intrinsically evil. In fact, he says nothing; he merely weeps.

Golding has given Ralph an adult's feelings and a hero's tragic awareness, while at the same time insisting Ralph is just a boy. But then, everyone on the island is a boy, including the savages. Just before their rescue, suddenly and cinematically, as in a dissolve, they revert to what they were when they landed on the island: kids. Golding, who often shifts point of view, presents them in the end from the perspective of the naval officer who knows nothing of their Dionysian behavior and sees Jack not as a Bacchant but as "a little boy with a black cap."

Ralph and Simon are by no means models of consistency. The last line of the novel has Ralph weeping for the darkness of the heart, the loss of innocence, and "the fall through the air of the true, wise friend called Piggy." Yet there was nothing about Ralph's behavior to indicate that he ever found Piggy wise or a friend. Piggy was an ally; to think of him as Ralph's friend is to ignore Ralph's early derision of him.

Simon's character is the novel's chief weakness. Simon is an amalgam of various types and strains. Like his namesake in the nursery rhyme, he is simple; he strikes others, including Ralph, as peculiar. He is also a Cassandra, whose prophecies are doomed to be ignored. To give him a spiritual aura, Golding inflicts him with what the ancients called the sacred disease—epilepsy. Simon is the classic case of one whose clairvoyance is compensation for physical suffering.

Simon has also been called a Christ-figure, not so much because he evokes Christ (his obviously Christian qualities are shared by saints) as because he is a sacrificial victim. Certainly no child in literature has been saddled with such a multimythic personality. Furthermore, he is also Golding's mouthpiece, for it is Simon who expresses, however inarticulately, the author's philosophy of evil. Simon alone confronts the Lord of the Flies, from whose gaze he intuits "an ancient, inescapable recognition"—namely, that "everything is a bad business." Simon knows that the reason for the dissolution of the island community, and for evil in general, is humankind's bedeviled nature. But that knowledge is itself destructive; once Simon admits it ("I know that"), there is no hope. The butterflies desert his covert, and the flies start swarming on him, as if he bears the mark of the beast—which he does, since he is later identified with it. To Golding, knowledge of evil brings evil on the knower, no matter how innocent that person may be.

In case anyone has missed the point, Golding adds another encounter between Simon and the pig's head in which the head speaks: "'You knew didn't you? I'm part of you? . . . I'm the reason why it's no go? Why things are what they are?'" (177) This time Simon faints because the "ancient, inescapable recognition" has been expressed so unequivocally.

The incident is gratuitous; it is as if Golding, uncertain that his readers would get the message, decided to enunciate it so there would be no misunderstanding. To do so, he uses a child; from a critical standpoint, he "uses" a character—a character who has already relayed the message to readers sensitive enough to comprehend it. It seems that Simon is Golding's scapegoat as well as the hunters'.

The incident is gratuitous for another reason. Simon's awareness of evil is made evident early in the novel. Like Ralph and Jack, Simon knows there is no beast; "maybe it's only us" (111) he suggests. To clarify his suggestion, he asks timidly, "What's the dirtiest thing there is?" Jack answers in a word of "one crude expressive syllable." The monosyllabic word is obviously "shit," which, at the time, Golding was too circumspect to use. In the context, periphrasis is out of place, but Golding later made up for his reticence, growing more explicit with the times.

The logic is elementary but depressing; if humans are the beast, then humans are shit—something Sweeney Todd, "the demon barber of Fleet Street" in Stephen Sondheim's eponymous musical drama, believes, for that is how he justifies avenging himself on the world.

The scene in which Simon made his suggestion, supplemented by the first encounter with the pig's head, would have been sufficient; together, they establish the two basic metaphors for evil: flies and excrement, so that the Lord of the Flies is the Lord of Dung, and what is true of the lord is true of his servants. Moreover, excrement is ubiquitous on the island. Eating fruit causes diarrhea, and the island is dotted with feces. The island, like everything in the novel, is a parody—a parody of the first garden, Eden, where the first sin was committed. The fruit is tainted by the first sin whose effects the boys, like all humanity, have inherited. The excrement they leave behind is a vestige of the primal sin.

It is precisely this kind of symbolism that has made *Lord of the Flies* such a teachable novel, to the extent that one can ignore Simon's unsatisfying characterization. The novel is a perfect illustration of the way the literal and metaphorical levels of a work complement each other since, in *Lord of the Flies,* the metaphorical level is a deepening of the literal. For those who find mythopoesis tough going, there are always the characters who are such identifiable types that, as one student observed, they could be found at camp.[11] For those capable of going beyond symbolism into irony and ambivalence, Golding facilitates the transition by using irony to underscore the symbolic action. The fire that was made by the reflection of light from Piggy's glasses goes out when Jack kills his first pig. When Jack prays for a sign from heaven, his prayer is answered in the form of the dead paratrooper. Finally, there are summary lines like "the dirtiest thing there is" and "I'm the reason why it's no go" which, as the novel moved into secondary school, were a godsend to students who had to locate the novel's central thought or the author's philosophy.

Lord of the Flies also affords an opportunity to test Golding's own interpretation of the novel and to decide whether one trusts the tale or the teller. In a 1962 lecture at the University of California at Los Angeles, Golding turned critic and interpreted the dead paratrooper as history that "won't lie down."[12] No doubt he meant that the paratrooper was another instance of humankind's irrational fears projected onto an object—a harmless object, at that. Golding apparently forgot that the paratrooper does lie down—literally—and can be laid down symbolically. Simon disentangles the parachute lines so the corpse does not jerk up and down; after Simon's death, the rain washes the corpse out to sea. Simon manages to get the corpse to "lie down," thus showing that the irrational can be put to rest; unfortunately, he never had the chance to announce his discovery to the others. Apparently even authors can misinterpret their work.

Finally, *Lord of the Flies* remains an excellent introduction to fable, myth, and allegory since it embodies features of each, although strictly speaking, it is none of them. It is a work whose foundation (or to use a favorite Golding word, cellar) is mythic; it has the moral purpose of fable and the symbolic linkings of allegory. It also has certain features in common with antiallegory, as defined by Northrop Frye in *Anatomy of Criticism.* Antiallegory is a peculiarly modern form that inverts the imagery of traditional allegory, so that instead of being exemplary and doctrinal, the imagery becomes ironic and paradoxical. Thus antiallegory is the reverse of classical allegory, which teaches that human nature is perfectible; antiallegory teaches the opposite, or, to use the words of the pig's head, that "it's no go." Antiallegory is merely another way of saying serious parody, which is perhaps the most accurate designation for the novel.

Chapter Three

Our Ancestral Ogres

Point of Departure

Golding considered *Lord of the Flies* "a realistic view of the Ballantyne situation";[1] he considers *The Inheritors* (1955) a realistic response to H. G. Wells. Golding's second novel continues to explore the end of innocence, this time from the point of view of a primitive family. Just as the author took exception to Ballantyne's optimism in *Lord of the Flies*, in *The Inheritors* he takes exception to another misguided belief— H. G. Wells's—that *homo sapiens sapiens* is evolution's crowning achievement. The novel's epigraph is from Wells's *Outline of History*; like a T. S. Eliot epigraph, the Wells quotation should be taken as Golding's point of departure:

We know little of the appearance of the Neanderthal man, but this . . . seems to suggest an extreme hairiness, an ugliness, or repulsive strangeness in his appearance over and above his low forehead, his beetle brows, his ape neck, and his inferior stature. . . . Says Sir Harry Johnston, in a survey of the rise of modern man in his *Views and Reviews*: "The dim racial remembrance of such gorilla-like monsters, with cunning brains, shambling gait, hairy bodies, strong teeth, and possibly cannibalistic tendencies, may be the germ of the ogre in folklore."[2]

Except for *Darkness Visible,* Golding has never shied away from discussing the genesis of his novels and is, in fact, quite explicit about the inspiration for *The Inheritors*:

Wells' *Outline of History* played a great part in my life because my father was a rationalist, and the *Outline* . . . was something he took neat. Well now, Wells' *Outline of History* is the rationalist's gospel *in excelsis,* I should think. I got this from my father, and by and by it seemed to me not to be large enough. It seemed to me to be too neat and slick. And when I re-read it as an adult I came across his picture of Neanderthal man, our immediate predecessors, as being the gross brutal creatures who were possibly the basis of the mythological bad man, whatever he may be, the ogre. I thought to myself that this is just absurd. What we're doing is externalizing our inside.[3]

Twenty years after the *Outline,* in *The Fate of Homo Sapiens,* Wells predicted the destiny of humanity, warning it to "adapt or perish." Education was the only answer; primitives, "low-browed and brutish" creatures, whose skulls imprisoned their brain, were destined to inhabit a world bereft of thought and culture. But *homo sapiens sapiens,* the "true" humans, the teachable animals, had minds that could be trained toward the good. Wells went further and insisted that humans had a solemn obligation to train their minds for that purpose.

Golding took issue with Wells. *Homo sapiens sapiens,* while educable, has a morally uneven history. One's belief in the inherent goodness of humankind is buoyed up by a Dante, a Shakespeare, or a Mozart; but there are also the Stalins and the Hitlers. To Golding, the rise of totalitarianism and the existence of death camps represent the species at its worst. Nor is humankind necessarily transfigured by education, as the cultivated Dr. Halde, the Nazi psychologist of *Free Fall,* proves. The specters of evil do not lie hidden in the nodes of the evolutionary chain; they dwell in the darkness of the heart.

Although *The Inheritors* is antirationalist, it is not polemical. The epigraph is only a terminus a quo for a novel that can be read on several levels, the least meaningful of which is "primitive—*si,* modern—*non.*" Golding has again chosen one of his skeletal themes, pitting one way of life against another and allowing the narrative to grow out of their clash. But as usually happens with works of bipolar design, the simpler the lines of construction, the greater the symbolic potential of the whole.

In any era, *The Inheritors* would be a tour de force; Golding has not only taken characters alien or even repellent to readers conditioned by rationalism and portrayed them sympathetically; he has also succeeded in recreating a lost society complete with language patterns that vividly capture the aconceptual nature of primitive thought. Golding's primitives think in pictures ("I have a picture"), a fact that seems obvious enough from the Wellsian epigraph; but when the characters elaborate on these pictures, they reveal something equally as precious as a mind—a racial memory, a childlike wonder, a creative imagination, or to use one of Golding's favorite words, "innocence."

To what extent such innocence is anthropologically valid is another matter. A novelist cannot be expected to portray primitive life with scholarly fidelity; still, critics have pointed out that a novel in which Neanderthals are replaced by *homo sapiens* is anthropologically unsound.[4] In fairness to Golding, neither the word "Neanderthal" nor "*homo sapiens*" appears in the novel, which is written from the characters' point of view. Golding, however, did promote this interpretation in interviews and essays when he implied that the Neanderthal and *homo sapiens* were distinct. Ironically, Golding knew enough cultural anthropology to realize that *homo sapiens neanderthalensis* was an early or perhaps a variant form of the modern human; thus the novel is about the absorption of *homo sapiens neanderthalensis* by *homo sapiens sapiens*.

The People

The eight-member family of *The Inheritors,* the last of its species, is portrayed, by and large, as Neanderthal. The "people," as its members are called, are ignorant of navigation; they use logs or dead trees to ford rivers and streams. On the other hand, they have mastered fire; they also take care of their old, and they bury their dead with offerings. Physically, Golding's "people" conjure up something even older than the Neanderthals. From the way they scurry about, play, and climb trees, they suggest some kind of hominoid primate—perhaps the orangutan who, oddly enough, may well be humankind's first cousin. Golding seems to be combining Neanderthal habits with hominoid behavior to create a composite of the forerunners of the modern human.

Golding's family migrates from winter to summer camping grounds. Although its members function as a closely knit group, relationships are, at first, difficult to ascertain. Recall the conch that rallied the boys in *Lord of the Flies,* thereby enabling Golding to introduce them; the disappearance of a log serves a similar function in *The Inheritors.* There is, however, a difference. Children may impose limitations on an author, but Neanderthals restrict an author to a primitive consciousness and to a point of view even more confining than a child's. Golding's methods, which are entirely valid and represent an ingenious way of entering a mind so radically different from our own, has prompted one critic to complain that "sometimes the reader does not know what is going on."[5]

Admittedly, this is an extreme reaction. Although Golding is focusing on a family, he does not introduce the members with tags and nonrestrictive clauses that would explain their relationships to one another. He cannot because the family does not think in terms of relationships. Golding's family is matriarchal and polygamous; the "old woman" is not so much wife or mother as the priestess of the mother goddess; similarly, men and women are not so much husbands and wives as mates. Gradually, the reader discovers that the eight-member family consists of the dying Mal; his wife, "the old woman"; Ha and Fa, apparently mates; Nil, who has recently given birth to "the new one"; Lok, who also possessed Fa as a mate; and Liku, Lok's daughter by Nil.

Golding demands much of the reader; nowhere is this more evident than on the first page of the novel. Lok, who develops into the protagonist and finally into a tragic figure, is carrying Liku on his shoulders. They are playing "piggy back." Liku is carrying the little Oa in such a way that it is under Lok's chin. One's first inclination is to regard the little Oa as an infant and wonder if Golding may not be straining credulity by including an infant in their romp. Then one reads that Liku puts the little Oa's head to her mouth; the little Oa is waved when the family sees an ice formation that is a natural symbol of their goddess. Later, the little Oa is fed meat, but one must remember that Liku is speaking: "I ate meat. And little Oa ate meat."[6]

The little Oa is a doll; children can, and do, speak of feeding their dolls. A work written from a primitive's perspective must be read closely. If it is, one readily sees that Golding is not playing games; there is no deception, but, on the other hand, there is no pandering. Since *The Inheritors* is the author's densest novel, it requires careful explication. Narrative, image, and symbol interpenetrate and interresonate; thus, taking the novel simply on the basis of plot or studying it purely for its imagery is like diverting the flow of water from the fields it is supposed to irrigate and letting it stagnate. If the explication seems laborious, one can only argue that Golding regards *The Inheritors* as his finest novel; yet many readers have despaired of getting beyond the first page. But if one does, the results are even more gratifying than discovering that there are no heroes in *Lord of the Flies*.

The Art of Concealing Art

A cursory reading of the opening pages of the novel might leave one with the impression that nothing of significance happens. The truth of the matter is that Golding has only dispensed with traditional exposition, preferring to weave the narrative around a matrix of images so that the plot will become as much a concatenation of images as of episodes. The initial image is one of carefree existence; then it is counterpointed with one of anxiety—the disappearance of a log by which the family always crosses the stream to reach its summer habitation.

Since at this point we are within Lok's consciousness, we share his dilemma. The picture of the log in his imagination has no corresponding object in reality. The memory and the reality, the picture and its lack of a referent, constitute the first episode of the novel. Once Golding has made the log part of the plot (done by investing the image with narrative value), he can use the log as a means of introducing the remaining members of the family by having each of them react to its disappearance in a different way. Lok responds like one emerging from sleep; Fa is suspicious, believing at first that Lok planned it as a joke; Liku is only interested in playing; Ha looks for intruders; finally, the distraught Nil, Mal, and the old woman appear. And so the clan has gathered.

Having progressed from image to episode, Golding then uses the episode to elicit sympathy for the family, soon revealed to be the last of its species. The disappearance of the log bodes ill. Newcomers have taken it; the "people's" world has been invaded. What will be lost is not just a species but a commonality, a oneness with nature that has enabled the "people" to be both individual and group because they have not yet evolved to a stage where matter and spirit, Apollonian and Dionysian are distinct. The "people" hear separately and collectively, racially and individually, with ears so attuned to the voice of nature that they can disentangle complexes of sound: "their ears as if endowed with separate life sorted the tangle of tiny sounds and accepted them, the sound of breathing, the sound of wet clay flaking and ashes falling in" (34).

What is truly tragic is that the "people" do not know what will be lost. Golding knows, and what the "people" cannot accomplish he can. He cannot arouse pity for them since they do not pity themselves; instead, he allows the "people" to manifest their integrity through actions that are characterized by a lack of guilt. The "people" are vegetarians; they eat meat only when an animal has already been killed. Thus they can justify eating it, as they do their eating a slain doe, because "there is no blame."

The "people" are united by the bond of cosmic sympathy; since they believe all life is interlinked, they believe all life is sacred. Thus killing for food is alien to them because it is the willful destruction of life.

While the people practice polygamy, they are sexually restrained. Uninhibited about their nakedness, they take biological differences for granted.

The "people's" harmony is also endearing. They are homeopathic—laughing together, weeping together. When Mal shivers, the others shiver with him; when one "has a picture," the others listen with closer attention, attempting to help out should his or her picture fail. When Lok plays the buffoon to amuse them, they laugh with him, applauding his antics; they know his limitations ("Lok has a mouthful of words and no pictures") and willingly give him the limelight he needs.

But every Eden has its apple and serpent and is doomed to be short-lived. Shadows begin to envelop the community, and the invasion of the New People is foreshadowed in an evening scene that is filled with presentiments of disaster. While the others sleep, Lok is restless; he senses "eyes watching him from the cliffs." He sniffs at unfamiliar odors, but the scents elude him. The episode reaches a descriptive and emotional climax with the rising of the moon amid fragments of cloud; moonbeams spread a silver glaze over nature like the lunar shroud that was woven for Simon in *Lord of the Flies*: "The moon rose slowly and almost vertically into a sky where there was nothing but a few spilled traces of cloud. The light crawled down the island and made the pillars of spray full of brightness. . . . It fell on the trees of the forest so that a scatter of faint ivory patches moved over the rotting leaves and earth. It lay on the river and the wavering weed-tails; and the water was full of tinsel loops and circles and eddies of liquid cold fire" (43).

No Man Is an Island (except Man)

Morally and topographically, *The Inheritors* recalls the world of *Lord of the Flies*. Instead of fruit- and meat-eaters, there are vegetarians and carnivores; instead of Apollonians and Dionysians, there are the prelapsarian "people"—humanity before the fall—and the postlapsarian moderns, humanity after the fall. The geography complements the dichotomy. The New People (who correspond to modern humans) live on an island shaped like a giant's leg. They live in isolation; there is no natural bridge to the island. Since the "people," like the Neanderthals, are not seafarers, they fear the island and also consider it an unnatural habitation. When Lok and Fa journey to the island in search of Liku and the New One, they cross on logs—dead trees, a fitting form of transportation to the isle of the dead where a religion of death is practiced.

In contrast, the "people's" summer habitation is an overhang, some-what like a monkey terrace, next to a waterfall, below which is the island. Golding's symbolism again derives from the setting, or rather from the landscape; he does not have to coax symbols out of nature to create analogies with the Fall. Just as at the end of the *Inferno* Dante rose above evil as time and hemispheres changed, so too does Golding imply that the "people" exist on a plane beyond evil by locating it below them—on the island. Thus the "people" have not yet fallen, although eventually they will. In one of Golding's most pregnant, most ambivalent lines, Lok replies to Fa, who tells him of her picture of crossing over to the island on a log: "But men cannot go over the fall like a log." At the end of the novel, the line takes on its fullest meaning as the New People go over the fall into a world they will dominate, while Fa, struck on the head by their witch doctor, goes over the fall also—but to her death. Like all of Golding's symbolism, the fall is tragically ambivalent. It is retroactive, affecting even those who were not products of it; it is omnipresent, its vestiges persisting even in the survivors.

To conclude that the moderns are victims of the Fall and that the primitives are victims of the moderns is to grasp only half of Golding's meaning. In a Golding novel, one meaning generates a counter mean-ing, so that no interpretation is exhaustive. Golding is clearly discour-aging a monolithic approach to his novel. While the protagonist-antagonist syndrome is tempting, in *The Inheritors* both species are the victims of a changing environment. In fact, the "people" would have died off anyway, even if the newcomers had never arrived.

The "people" remember a time when it was endless summer, but they must adapt to a shifting climate; this they find difficult to do. Moreover, food is scarce; the bees no longer make the honey the "peo-ple" once ate. The New People have a similar problem; the dwindling supply of meat has made it necessary for them to cannibalize. They no longer have the strength to fell trees; thus they had to steal the log for their fire.

Although decay is everywhere, it does not materialize suddenly. Golding builds it up gradually, so that by the end of the novel, the humans' position ("What else could we have done?") seems more a statement of tragic inevitability than a question. Golding also builds gradually, but inexorably, to the realization that we, the inheritors, have cannibalized our ancestors—literally, as the novel attests, but symbolically as well, in the sense that we have reduced them to bones and artifacts. But that should not come as a surprise after *Lord of the Flies*; what children do in their way, adults do in theirs.

One by one, the "people" are reduced in number until, of the eight, only Lok, Fa, and the New One are left; and finally, only the "new one." First, Ha disappears while gathering wood with Nil; he is last seen smiling at someone on the cliff. One must assume he is killed and roasted, for all that remains of him is "a dirty smudge in the earth where the fire had been" (103). Mal, who has grown progressively ill with pneumonia, dies and is buried with a simple ritual carried out by people who accept death as the inevitable consequence of life. Then the New People "without pictures in their heads" appear. One of them abducts Liku; when Lok tries to rescue her, the abductor shoots a poisoned arrow at him, although it is never described as such. To a Neanderthal, there is no such object. The arrow resembles the closest thing in nature with which he is familiar—a twig; that is precisely how Golding describes it. Lok smells it, and lacking a word for poison, associates the odor with "bitter berries [one] must not eat" (106).

Next, Nil and the old woman are killed, and the 'new one" is taken away. At the end of chapter 5, Lok stares down at the water where his mother's body lies. The emotional effect is stunning because of the absence of anything resembling grief or lamentation. Lok's attitude toward the old woman when she was alive was one of love mingled with awe; appropriately, his last look at her is poignant but restrained: "Her eyes swept across the bushes, across his face, looked through him without seeing him, rolled away and were gone" (109).

With the reduction of the family to Lok and Fa, *The Inheritors* reaches midpoint. The last half of the novel is a moral and symbolic reversal of the first, for everything about the New People is the diametric opposite of the Neanderthals. The New People or humans are not broadnosed like the Neanderthals; their nostrils are narrow. The humans' eyebrows and lips are thin; in fact, everything about them suggests emaciation. Their waists are "wasp thin"; their women have sagging breasts. The men tire easily; they are "dream men," acting robotically and barely able to bring their canoes up on the shore.

In contrast to the Neanderthals' matriarchal structure, the humans have adopted a patriarchal system in which the women are regarded as inferiors. The humans are also belligerent; they drink wine from a wine skin that, when it is poured, looks like a urinating animal. While the Neanderthals were polygamous but sexually circumspect, the humans are promiscuous but blatantly so. Yet the humans are ashamed of their nakedness and, in the absence of fig leaves, cover their loins with deerskin.

Just as the boys of *Lord of the Flies* worshiped a pig's head, the humans worship a stag. The main difference, however, is that the pig had not yet evolved into a totem animal although, if the boys had been older, it might have. The stag, on the other hand, is a totem animal, and with that evolution has come a religion thriving on fear, guilt, mutilation, and cannibalization. When the witch doctor decides that a human sacrifice is needed either to placate the stag or to obtain some favor from it, lots are drawn, and the winner loses his finger. The humans do not cannibalize their own; they mutilate them. Even the Bacchants had not sunk to cutting off their extremities.

Gradually, one learns that the humans have names, although unlike the names of the Neanderthals, theirs are less simple and less euphonious. Golding, the careful craftsman, has seen to it that the humans are the reverse of the Neanderthals in every way. Mal's opposite is Marlan, the witch doctor who keeps the tribe enslaved with the stag religion which, in turn, keeps him in power. The negative of Ha/Nil is Vivani, Marlan's chattel (one hesitates to call her a mate since the humans treat women as objects); she is lust-driven, flabby, but not wholly evil, as one discovers at the end. The reverse of Liku is Tanakil, to whom Liku is given as a plaything on a leash; Tanakil is the daughter of Tuami and Twal (the latter identified, for some reason, only at the end). Lok's double is Tuami, an artist who gradually replaces Lok as a sentient center so that the conclusion and, in fact, the entire experience is viewed from his perspective.

Viewing the Fall

Until that replacement happens, and for it to happen, Golding effects a spectacular change in point of view. First he shows how the newcomers look through the Neanderthal's eyes. Golding had suggested earlier that they might first seek to imitate the newcomers. To acquire the qualities of the *other*, one mimics *other*. Lok's initial impressions of the humans are of predatory, snarling, snakelike beings. As Jack in *Lord of the Flies* tried to get an idea of his prey by imitating it, Lok does the same with humans. This imitation is based, however, on scents and instincts, not on direct experience or eyewitness accounts; Lok has not yet encountered the alien culture.

To bring both species into contact and to shift point of view as imperceptibly as possible, Golding grafts the images of tree and island onto a narrative incident—Lok's attempt to rescue Liku and the "new one" from the humans. When Lok and Fa reach the island, they climb a tree from which they view the stag ritual and its aftermath. The incident offers Golding a chance to expand the Eden metaphor, giving it several connotations. First, one thinks of the Tree of the Knowledge of Good and Evil in the Garden of Eden. In climbing the tree, Lok is taking his first steps toward understanding the humans; the tree gives him a vantage point for observing their behavior.

The tree, however, is an ambivalent symbol; in the *Bacchae,* it was from a tree that Pentheus witnessed the Dionysian ritual. The view from the tree makes it impossible for the viewer to return to what he was before. What Lok sees is human behavior at its worst: mutilation, drunkenness, loveless sex, and greed (Marlan's eating the meat that Lok had thrown into the clearing for Liku). But there is one incident Lok does not see because Fa, in her terror, holds him so closely that he cannot see his daughter being cannibalized.

To continue the ambivalent perspective that governs the novel, if good can come from evil, then something can be learned from this display of depravity: the impact of the fall is immeasurable. Like Dante's Old Man of Crete, the fall is Janus-faced; it looks forward and backward, affecting all people regardless of their anthropological designation. Since Golding juxtaposes the Neanderthals and the humans by placing them in the same location, he is arguing that original sin, the legacy of the Fall, is retroactive, and that its effects are ubiquitous. The New People are the immediate heirs of Adam's curse, yet they have projected it onto the Neanderthals, whom they regard as ogres. Thus they prevent the Neanderthals from traveling up the river, therefore over the waterfall. If the Neanderthals have been prevented from journeying over the fall, they have also been prevented—symbolically—from transcending it. The New People have merely transferred their sin to their ancestors, making it the sin of humankind and not just the sin of *homo sapiens sapiens.* Moreover, they have denied salvation to their ancestors by regarding them as subhuman.

The Fall, then, is universal, retroactive, and temporal; it extends into the past, the future, and the present. If the humans have fallen, so can the Neanderthals. All the Neanderthals must do is reverse what they had been doing and change their morals, dietary habits, and manner of thought; become carnivores instead of vegetarians, wine- instead of water-drinkers, promiscuous instead of polygamous (polygamy and promiscuity are by no means synonymous to Neanderthals), and conceptual instead of instinctive.

The last is the most difficult to achieve because it occurs in stages; yet Lok achieves it when, as Golding observes with sardonic wordplay, "Lok discovered like." The first indication that the mind has gone beyond mere sense perception occurs when it begins to differentiate— to compare and contrast. For Lok, this means forsaking metaphor for simile. Lok originally thought metaphorically; when he saw some of the humans, he did not compare them with trees that he knew; he equated them with those trees, calling them by the trees' names: Chestnut, Pine-tree. Then Lok learns that humans are not trees but can be treelike. And to complete the irony, he is in a tree when he learns his first lesson in epistemology.

Once Lok discovers the simile, there is no stopping him: "The people are like honey trickling down from a crevice in the rock. . . . The people are like honey in the round stones, the new honey that smells of dead things and fire" (195). Comparative thought brings him to a conclusion too profound for him ever to realize its significance: "They are like the river and the fall, they are a people of the fall; nothing stands against them." Lok does not know why he has compared the humans to the river and the fall, yet he drops the comparison when he calls them "a people of the fall." They are like the river and the fall because, unlike the Neanderthals, they are navigators. But they are not *like* a people of the fall; they *are* a people of the Fall. This is classic irony—saying something that is as true on the primary level of meaning as it is on the secondary, but intending only the primary. Not knowing the meaning of the Fall, Lok cannot possibly understand what he has said; but knowing a particular fall, the one beneath which lies the island of the New People, he can make a comparison that is equally applicable to the "first fall."

Lok's final analogy indicates that he can perceive not only differences but also similarities between his people and the humans: "They are like Oa." Oa was the Neanderthals' Magna Mater or Great Mother. If the humans are like Oa, they are both creative and destructive. The Neanderthals have witnessed examples of Oa's destructiveness: the great fire, the radical change of climate. Yet they have also known her beneficence "when it was summer all year round and the flowers and fruit hung on the same branch"(35).

If the humans are like Oa, they have two sides. This should also be true of the Neanderthals, who are also like Oa. Golding, however, does not pursue this point because he has made the humans the dark side of the Neanderthals, thereby reversing the traditional view. Still, to present a balanced picture of *homo sapiens sapiens,* Golding has Lok witness human artistry as well as human barbarism. Lok marvels at Tuami's art—necklaces of shells and a doll that, significantly, he calls an Oa since it reminds him of Liku's "little Oa." But the humans' doll is so lifelike that it almost looks dead. By adding that one feature to the doll, Golding gently pulls the rug out from under the critic who thinks he or she has divined his meaning. Golding's meanings are slippery. The doll may look dead because it is emblematic of its culture. On the other hand, the detail is too perfect for the doll to look alive—an indication that humans are capable of producing something "correctly cold," as Pope would say. Still, it is art, and Lok is entranced by it.

Lok has experienced something like Aristotelian deduction; he has progressed from sensible particulars (wolf, snake, river, fall) to a universal conclusion: they are like Oa. There is one last step: the application of this new knowledge, this new form of reasoning, to himself. When Lok drinks the New People's wine, the equivalent of the forbidden fruit, he exclaims: "I am one of the new people" (204). This is the kind of knowledge that the great tragedies inculcate: knowledge of the self and of humankind. Lok has achieved it but only in words; he had the experience but missed the meaning, as T. S. Eliot would have put it. Although Lok will not live long enough to understand the implications of being human, he has at least gone through the motions.

Once Lok admits to being one of the New People, there is no possibility of the novel's continuing from his point of view. Thus the point of view changes in a spectacular shift of perspective, so that the action, which had been witnessed from one point of view, is now witnessed not from another but from the same-as-other; or to use Golding's words, from the point of view of "Lok-other." By a shift of consciousness, Golding brings the Neanderthals and the humans together if not into a single entity, then into a single point of view. The superimposition and then absorption of visions is almost cinematic, recalling the moment in Ingmar Bergman's *Persona* when the director merges the faces of Alma and Elisabet to show that they are halves of one personality.

Golding is bound by his own transformation; thus Lok's death must be described as Lok-other would experience it and as Lok-other would observe it. Lok, once a he, becomes an it; once a man, he becomes a "red creature" indescribable in gender or other terms that are even remotely human. The creature trots, scrambles, sniffs, and staggers: "It was a strange creature, smallish, and bowed" (218–29). When Lok approaches the image that the New People have left, he does so with the curiosity of a dog eyeing a toy replica of itself. Since Lok cannot comprehend his fate, he simply weeps, and his tears fall upon a withered leaf. Lok's death is canine; to put it brutally, he dies like a dog. He begins "to scramble in the earth" and with "the right forepaw" digs up a female-shaped root, the emblem of the goddess Oa, to whom he then returns. He approaches the waterfall where he assumes the position of a fetus and awaits absorption into Oa's womb. Lok's return to the mother goddess is signaled by the collapse of the ice formations, now melted by the sun. A new era dawns, but not without thundering chords that reverberate through the mountains and out toward the sea.

The final chapter must be read as closely as the first; both are like bookends enclosing Golding's single-volume history of humanity. *The Inheritors* begins and ends with a family. The new family, however, is not a group that shares a common identity; it comprises a ruthless despot, Marlan; a potential murderer, Tuami; a deranged child, Tanakil; and an adulterous mother, Vivani. They have inherited the earth from Lok and will proceed to sow it accordingly. Although a sunburst christens their journey, it is not a voyage into the light but into darkness; as such, it can only be painted in chiaroscuro. At the very end of the novel, Tuami gazes at the line of darkness along the horizon, but "he could not see if the line of darkness had an ending." Both *Lord of the Flies* and *The Inheritors* conclude with the word "darkness," Golding's mot juste for the human condition.

The Novel as Prose Poem

Of all Golding's novels, *The Inheritors* is the most successful at crossing the line of demarcation between poetry and artistic prose. In addition to the edenic imagery, there is also Golding's cinematic use of light and darkness to create a world roofed in by shadow, occasionally shot with sun. Imagery, however, is inseparable from character; the Neanderthal mind is similar to the shadowy paradise in which the "people" live—misty, adumbrated by undefined memories, and sometimes illuminated by pictures.

Much of the action takes place at night, often by a smoking fire. The first chapter ends with a sunset and "shadows . . . racing through the gap towards the terrace." The sun sets frequently in *The Inheritors*, casting an aura of mystery and foreboding. Lok's premonition of "something else" on the island occurs in eerie moonlight. Mal is illuminated by the setting sun "so that shadows stretched from him to the other end of the fire" (63–64). He is also buried at night. As Lok and Fa go in search of Liku, "their bodies wove a parallel skein of shadows" (118). They possess "night sight" and can therefore make their way through the underbrush to the habitation of the New People. Lok dies in twilight that turns his red body gray and blue. Significantly, the novel ends with Tuami looking at an unending line of darkness.

Golding considers *The Inheritors* his finest novel, although, as we shall see, his true masterpiece is *Rites of Passage*. Still, one can understand his fondness for it. *The Inheritors* is a personal work, harking back to the author's boyhood. In his essay "Digging for Pictures," which provides an even better background for *The Inheritors* than Wells's *Outline,* Golding describes how, as a youngster, he did some excavating and came upon bones of a family from "the days of innocence."[7] He then noticed something that might have been the head of a doll—no doubt the inspiration for "the little Oa." Golding's first dig left an indelible impression on him; equally strong was Golding's memory of the bulldozer that covered over his excavation while making a runway, causing a "prehistoric murder."

One can readily understand how a child's initial confrontation with the prehistoric past might have supplied the first strands of a web eventually woven into a novel. Contact with those bones had "taken something of me with them," Golding claims; yet the contact was reciprocal, for the bones gave Golding the basis of one of his best novels. The encounter with the bones may also have given Golding his first insight into the nature of innocence which, etymologically, is harmlessness. Conversely, knowledge of the opposite—of the ability to harm—signals the end of innocence. One has the feeling from "Digging for Pictures" that Golding lost his innocence when he saw his newly found world of bones and artifacts entombed forever by a bulldozer. One also has the feeling that the experience gave the young Golding an appreciation of primitive thought as something richly pictorial. As Golding notes in the essay, "history is not diagrams—however accurate—but pictures." Lok and his family can only think in pictures ("I have a picture") that contain the history of their race and become externalized in artifacts.

Although in *The Inheritors* Golding is still preoccupied with the two worlds-two wisdoms dichotomy, his portrayal of it is more complex than in *Lord of the Flies* because the doubling is more successful. While Lok and Tuami are doubles, Tuami, even though he survives Lok, is as pitiful as the doomed Neanderthal. Lok has at least returned to the womb of the mother goddess; Tuami must embark on a perilous journey in a *bateau ivre* against an horizon that can promise no light. In their journey into darkness, the New People require as much compassion as the Neanderthals; they are, after all, ourselves, and the final chapter is our mirror. Tuami realizes that progress always occurs at another's expense, but "what else could we have done?" (227). He would like to murder Marlan, his rival for Vivani's affections, and begins to sharpen a piece of ivory into a point. But he soon stops: "Who would sharpen a point against the darkness of the world?" (231).

Vivani, who may have played the whore earlier with Tuami, can still be maternal to the Neanderthal child on board, even though it is a "red devil." This specter of the past may frighten her, but she does not deny it a mother's affection: "Hesitating, half-ashamed, with that same frightened laughter, she bent her head, cradled him with her arms and shut her eyes" (230–31).

The Neanderthals are not the heroes, nor are the New People the villains of the novel. If the New People are the "true men," as Wells called moderns in the *Outline,* if they are supposed to tower over the rest of creation, they should be capable of using their intellect to quell their dark, demonic urges. Yet the opposite is true: the New People are less able to master them than the Neanderthals. Each rung on the evolutionary ladder brings additional knowledge, but always at a price.

It is significant that the humans take a Neanderthal child with them on their ominous voyage. They regard it as a "red devil," for that is how *homo sapiens sapiens* tends to regard his ancestors: *they* were the bedeviled ones, the cannibals, the idolators—not he. But the real devil, the real ogre, lies within the darkness of the heart. *Homo sapiens neanderthalensis* may be the shadow self of *homo sapiens sapiens*; or, as Golding implies, it may be the opposite. Regardless, it is impossible to separate the shadow from the one who casts it.

Chapter Four

After the First Death

Death and Transmogrification

In *Pincher Martin* (1956) Golding attempted a blend of the adventure tale, which requires straightforward narration, with a series of flashbacks or "memory scenes," which are fragmentary and allusive. The plot itself is easily summarized; *Pincher Martin* is the story of Christopher Hadley Martin, the sole survivor of a British warship, the *Wildebeeste,* that is torpedoed in the Atlantic during World War II. At the beginning Martin is apparently drowning; at the end a British officer recovers his body. Between the drowning and the recovery, however, a miracle seems to have occurred. Martin, saved by his life belt, is cast up on a rock island where he recalls experiences of his past life and where he magnificently combats hunger, sickness, and the elements in a determined effort to survive

Although the recovery of the body seems to subvert the whole point of the novel (which is largely concerned with Martin's struggle to exist), there is no narrative inconsistency if one remembers that Martin has died within minutes of the torpedoing and that the major part of the book describes the afterlife he undergoes. The beginning is understandable only in terms of the end, and the novel's movement is like the calculated tracing of a circle that takes on intelligibility when the curve is finally closed. The reader must retrace the curve of the circle from its starting point and view the end in terms of the beginning.

There is no doubt that on the very first page Golding is describing a drowning: "When the air had gone with the shriek, water came in to fill its place—burning water, hard in the throat and mouth as stones that hurt." Martin then seems to kick off his boots and inflate his lifelbelt, blowing "regularly into the tube until the lifebelt rose."[1] In the last chapter, Mr. Campbell, the Scot who finds Martin's body, remarks: "Those are wicked things, those lifebelts. They give a man hope when there is no longer any call for it" (207). Finally, the novel's last line makes it clear that Martin did not survive the torpedoing: "You saw the body. He didn't even have time to kick off his seaboots."

Although *Pincher Martin* has a discernible structure (the drowning, the aftermath, the recovery), it is a mistake to dwell solely on its narrative framework. Golding is not writing a melodrama; if he were, episodes would form a narrative that provided its own explanation. Golding's narrative is like a scaffold—necessary for construction but removable upon completion. The reader must first adhere to the details of the plot and accept Martin's presence on a rock island in the middle of an ocean. In fact, Golding facilitates such acceptance by stressing the physical and the tactile: the character touches moist objects and cracks mussel shells. At the end of the novel, the reader can stand outside the narrative and view it as a vehicle for metaphor. Again, Golding makes it easy: the rock island remains literal but can also be seen as a symbol, as a projection of Martin's petrified nature. What was literal in the reading becomes symbolic in the analysis.

Unfortunately, some have felt cheated by the ending. If so, they should remember that Golding is not playing a joke but rather jolting the casual reader into a state of moral awareness. Furthermore, one must not forget that before he entered the Royal Navy, Martin was an actor; and that the roles he played in civilian life were consistent with his character. When he was cast as Greed in a morality play, everyone, including the producer and his wife, agreed it was typecasting, especially for someone "born with his mouth and his flies open and both hands out to grab" (120). Other roles in Martin's self-mirroring repertoire include the misogynistic psychopath, Danny, in Emlyn Williams's *Night Must Fall*; the sybaritic Algernon in Oscar Wilde's *Importance of Being Earnest*; the superficial Freddy of Shaw's *Pygmalion*; Demetrius in Shakespeare's *Midsummer Night's Dream*; and although his role in Congreve's *Way of the World* is unspecified (it was probably Mirabell), it is easy to imagine Martin's substituting a leer for the wit of the Restoration comedy.

Golding has even written stage directions for Martin. In chapter 12, there is an encounter between Martin and his friend Nathaniel. Just before the ship is torpedoed, Martin sees Nat leaning on the rail. He is repelled by everything Nathaniel represents, especially his piety and his chaste love for Mary Lovell, who, to Martin, is merely an object of lust. Nat suggests Nathaniel, the Israelite in whom there is no guile (John 1:47); the symbolism of Mary Lovell's name is obvious—perhaps too much so. Martin cannot distinguish between the guileless and the virginal; he hopes that by destroying the former, he can blot the other out of his mind.

The Novelist as Stage Director

At this point Golding enters the action as omniscient narrator (or better, director), plotting the action with a pace that grows increasingly faster and giving his protagonist the proper staging to carry him through the scene. First Martin dismisses all witnesses. The directions read: "Feet descending the ladder. . . . Ham it a bit. Casual saunter to the port side. Pause" (185–86). Martin is then to cross to the voice pipe and cry, "Hard a starboard for Christ's sake" on the supposition that Nat will be swept off the rail. Again he is given the necessary staging: "Scramble to the binnacle, fling yourself at the voice pipe, voice urgent." Ironically, the order coincides with the torpedoing, but Martin feels no regret: "And it was the right bloody order!" (186).

When he uses the lifebelt to give himself an enema, he does it with the mixture of realism and fantasy that characterizes so much of the novel. Defecation is done to a scenario that calls for music from Tchaikovsky, Wagner, and Holst. One is to imagine something like Walt Disney's *Fantasia,* with swirling colors and extravagantly romantic music, punctuated by a blast from Martin's bowels. The setting is supplied for him; he has merely to stand within it and perform.

As soon as Martin is washed up on a rock island, he begins to play a role he had never performed onstage—the Odyssean hero, polytropic, wily, and indestructible. He finds his own food—mussels and anemones—suffers ptomaine poisoning from them, and proceeds to construct his own world with all of Ralph's tidy logic: "I call this place the Look-out. That is the Dwarf. The rock out there under the sun where I came swimming is Safety Rock. . . . On the south side where the strap-weed is, I call Prospect Cliff" (84). To put a label on one's environment is to control it, and Martin uses this logic to dispel his fear of the unknown. A self-conscious rationalism, however, does not satisfy him; soon he becomes aware that he is trying to avoid the realization that the island is not what it should be.

Golding allows Martin to attempt roles he could never have played in life. Chapter 13 is a bravura mad scene that would have been completely beyond the capabilities of Christopher Martin, juvenile lead. There is one caveat: Martin the shipwrecked figure differs at times from Martin the conceited actor. One must always keep in mind who the *real* Martin was. Although Golding has supplied biographical data, he does so in a series of fragmented memory scenes presented without any chronological order.

Reminiscence can be a clear and articulate device, as it is in Tennessee Williams's *Glass Menagerie* in which the narrator, Tom Wingfield, recalls scenes of his family life in St. Louis with remarkable clarity. Golding, on the other hand, is not asking the reader to enter the mind of someone who is sufficiently detached from the past to view it objectively; he demands that the reader plunge into the psyche of a lifeless man. The memory scenes in *Pincher Martin* are at first difficult to comprehend. Names appear out of nowhere: Pete, Helen, Nathaniel. Golding is telling a conventional tale in an unconventional way; thus he cannot use the traditional means of introducing characters. The seeming lack of clarity in these episodes is not faulty technique; they are the half-in-light, half-in-shadow recollections of a man whose memory continues after death, although it is far from perfect.

Nevertheless, a clear picture of Christopher Martin emerges from the memory scenes. His entire life has been devoted to consuming people. Martin is obsessed with eating, but of a special kind: "Eating women, eating men, crunching up Alfred" (90). His theater friends regard him as a parasite. Pete the producer recounts a tale about the preparation of a Chinese delicacy. A fish is placed in a tin box; soon maggots consume the fish, then one another, until one maggot alone emerges. Pincher is the triumphant maggot who cries with the exultation of a victorious child, "I'm a bigger maggot than you are" (153).

Even the protagonist's name is suggestive of his character. On the one hand, he is Christopher Martin; like his namesake, the third-century saint, he is also making a precarious journey across the water as a spiritual preparation. On the other, he is a Martin in the Royal Navy where all Martins are nicknamed "Pincher," just as every Mullins in the American army is "Moon Mullins." On still another level, he is *Pincher* Martin—Greed, the successful maggot—constantly grasping at whatever comes within his reach.

Within the course of the novel he seduces two women, rapes another, and engages in a "crude and unsatisfactory" experiment in homosexuality. In one memory scene he reenacts a bedroom farce with Sibyl and Alfred. He then proceeds to take his producer's wife, Helen, as his mistress. Concomitant with his need to satisfy his ego with people is the desire to destroy whatever is his opposite—Nathaniel, whom he seeks to murder, and Mary, whom he rapes.

Nathaniel is sketchily drawn, as indeed are all the characters in the memory scenes. Still, Golding has given him the most important words in the novel. Like Simon, Nathaniel is a mystic; like Simon, he has transcended the mundane in an environment not especially conducive to spirituality. Nat, however, is more articulate; while he may be a grown-up Simon, the maturing process has made all the difference between a child who must confront evil in a state of mute understanding and a man who has retained his childhood innocence but who can speak convincingly about the four last things: death, judgment, heaven, and hell.

Nat has a twofold function in the novel; he is the author's mouthpiece conveying a philosophy of death in a form far more poetic than that of the typical catechism. Nat believes one must achieve the ability to die *into* heaven, as if heaven were a state after life into which one passes in the same way one passes from childhood to adulthood—in a smooth, unbroken crossing. "Take us as we are now and heaven would be sheer negation. Without form and void. You see? A sort of black lightning, destroying everything that we call life—" (183).

More important, Nat is Martin's warner, a type of character common in Greek tragedy (Haemon in *Antigone,* Cadmus in the *Bacchae*). On two occasions in speaking of eternity, Nat indicates what will happen to Martin if he does not prepare himself for "dying into heaven." In the first, he feebly prophesies Martin's death; but because he is a visionary motivated by love and suffering, Nat cannot finish the sentence: "because in only a few years—" (71). The enraged Martin does complete the sentence, but in defiance and rage that such words should be uttered against himself, a personification of the life force. When Nat again speaks of life as a preparation for eternity, he alludes to the "black lightning" that will destroy those who pattern an afterlife on their own natures. Christopher Martin is such a person and, prophetically, is struck by black lightning.

What has been described thus far is the Martin of the memory scenes, the Martin of the past who lied and seduced his way through life. One must now consider the Martin who grapples with epic indignities on the rock island.

The Bound Promethean

The Martin on Rockall, the name he has given to his island home, belongs to the realm of myth. Definitions of myth are almost as numerous as its definers, but it is generally agreed that, as a critical term, it refers to a subject that is so sublimated that it is recognizable to everyone: "Myth is a dreamlike narrative in which the individual's cen-

tral concerns are united with society, time and the universe."[2] Thus
Martin on Rockall strikes a responsive chord in anyone familiar with
"survival literature," from the *Odyssey* to the most recent nuclear holo-
caust films such as *The Day After* and *Testament*. Features common to
survival narratives are present in *Pincher Martin*: humans versus the
elements, in search of food and shelter, and attempting to inject some
sort of order into chaos. But here the similarities end; Golding has
gone far beyond the survival narrative into the realm he has coopted—
parody, particularly mythic parody, in which Martin is contrasted with
the heroes of antiquity. Just before he is struck by the apocalyptic black
lightning, Martin cries, "I am Atlas. I am Prometheus" and again,
"Ajax! Prometheus!"

It would be easy to pass over these names as maniacal ravings, but
Golding, who uses an economy of words to achieve his effects, is not
embellishing his tale with classical allusions. The parallels are apt. In
ancient mythology, Atlas was punished for his role in the rebellion of
the Titans by being forced to hold up the heavens with his head and
hands. Like his Greek counterpart, Martin is limited to the confines
of a rock world, hemmed in by earth and sky. Ajax, the Greek warrior
in the *Iliad,* yearned for Achilles' armor, only to lose it to Odysseus;
then Ajax went mad and in his frenzy killed a flock of sheep, imagining
that they were the Greek leaders. In the final part of the novel, Martin
also goes "mad" in the sense of playing a mad scene that is really an
attempt to dispel his growing fear that the whole experience may be
delusive and he is indeed dead. To distinguish between Ajax's madness,
which was real, and Martin's, which is feigned, Golding allows Martin
to play *King Lear,* not the title role but that of the bastard Edgar, who
disguises himself as a madman and assumes the voice and manner of a
bedlamite (act 2, scene 3): "There was still a part that could be
played—there was the Bedlamite, Poor Tom." (177–78). Golding has
even gone so far as to invent verses reminiscent of the Shakespearean
tragedy: *"Rage, roar, and spout! / Let us have wind, rain, hail, gouts of
blood / Storms and tornadoes."*

Martin's roles reflect Golding's brand of symbolism, which is an
amalgam of irony, ambivalence, and paradox; thus the roles have multiple associations. If Martin can play one Titan, he can play another; if
he can play Atlas, he can play the brother of Atlas, Prometheus, the
Titan whom Zeus had chained to a cliff because he stole fire to aid
humankind. When Prometheus refused to tell Zeus the name of the
mortal who might someday overthrow him, he was swallowed up by

an earthquake amid thunder and lightning. Martin also defies God, who, like Zeus in Aeschylus's *Prometheus Bound,* assumes a form appropriate to the occasion. Just as Zeus appeared as thunder and lightning in Aeschylus, God appears as a seaman in Golding. God the Sailor is unusual in another respect: he looks like Martin. Just as the myths have been inverted and reversed, so too has God, who seems to be made in the human image, not the other way around. Even in death Martin inverts tradition.

In his defiance of Zeus, Prometheus at least spoke with poetic eloquence:

> In face of this I defy the flame
> Of the flickering tongue of the lightning flash.
> Let it strike two-forked, let the thunder crash,
> Let the wild typhoon and the hurricane
> Disrupt the space of the sky. Let shock
> Of air imprisoned blast rock from rock
> And tear the infernal roots apart
> Till the whole earth quake to its very heart,
> . . . .
> Whatever the peril, the doom, the pain,
> Self-existent I still remain.
> Zeus's hand can never destroy me.[3]

By contrast, Martin sounds illiterate. "I spit on your compassion," he screams. In a magnificent parody of *Prometheus Bound,* black lightning sunders earth from sky as Martin shrieks: "I shit on your heaven!"(200). However, it is a silent shriek, emanating from a mouth that can emit no sound.

Martin's exit role is that of the blasphemer, the God-defier. Although Golding does not specify the role, it is clearly a conflation of two mythological figures, "the lesser Ajax" and Capaneus. The "lesser Ajax"—not to be confused with the Telamonian Ajax who committed suicide—forced the virgin priestess Cassandra away from her temple and raped her. Shipwrecked on his homeward journey from Troy, he managed to swim ashore where he boasted that he had saved himself despite the gods. His arrogance infuriated Poseidon, the sea deity, who killed him by hurling the rock on which he stood into the sea.

Capaneus was also guilty of what Dante called violence against God. When he was scaling the walls of Thebes, he boasted that even Zeus could not stop him. Zeus indeed stopped him by striking him dead with a thunderbolt which, according to Statius who recounts the incident in the *Thebaid*, left his shield blackened—perhaps the source of Golding's black lightning.

Clearly these classical prototypes were not arbitrarily chosen; lightning figured prominently in the fates of Prometheus, the lesser Ajax, and Capaneus either as a manifestation of divine power or as a means of destruction. The classical prototypes are also facets of Martin's synthetic personality, which is made up of myths that are either inverted or parodied. Layers of mythic dimension have gone into the formation of Christopher Martin on Rockall. He is a manufactured hero, not a born one. Since he has not been created for heroism, his only claim to stature is to enact it.

What has been manufactured, however, can be dismantled. This is what happens not only to Martin but also to his island, which is a metaphorical extension of himself. First, the mouth that screamed obscenities at the Deity ceases to exist; all that remains is a center— Martin's id fantastically conceived in the form of a void with claws, as if a lobster were to vanish, leaving only its appendages behind. Thus, it is not the mouth that blasphemes but the center crying "wordlessly" out of the hate-knotted bowels of Martin's emptiness. As Martin metamorphoses, so does the setting. Just as a slow dissolve returned the savages to scruffy boys in *Lord of the Flies,* a similarly cinematic transformation occurs in *Pincher Martin*: the island contracts into a two-dimensional painted backdrop of the sort found in amateur theatricals.

Golding's Law of Symbolic Retribution

There are probably those who feel that the novel should have ended at this point, and not with the recovery of Martin's body. Nevertheless, since *Pincher Martin* is a theatre piece, the ending is apropos. Artists do not trick the public, and there is no doubt that Golding is an artist. The reader may have been mildly deceived, but the deception has been skillfully wrought. Golding has left several clues about the nature of Martin's death. First, there has obviously been a drowning, as even a cursory reading of the first page reveals. Golding has vividly described the separation of soul and body, although his escatology is not quite so simple. Drowning has only brought about a temporary severance of spirit and matter; the essence of Christopher Martin—a snarl—remains: "Could he have controlled the nerves of his face or could a face have been fashioned to fit the attitude of his consciousness where it lay

suspended between life and death that face would have worn a snarl"
(8).

Golding is working out of a Dantean premise, which is really a
poetic Thomism: the state of mind in which one dies is carried over
into the afterlife. What continues there, at least in Dante's conception,
is a metaphorical reincarnation of the self. Thus gluttons lie in garbage, sodomites roam a burning plain, thieves are continually undergoing transformation and so forth. Similarly, Martin carries his essence
over to the next world. Drowning cannot obliterate an essence; what
endures of Martin is his spiritual core, a muscularly contorted view of
the world—a snarl. For the sake of the fictional convention that does
not allow characters to function as disembodied spirits, the snarl is
humanized. Since the person is morally petrified, the setting must be
read as a metaphor of the person—a rock island; since the person is all
rock, the island is Rockall.

It would not be sufficient for the reader alone to know that Martin
is in a Dantean afterlife; the protagonist must also be aware of it.
Dante's dead know they are dead. Yet someone like Martin, who is all
id, wards off that realization just as in life he ignored the inevitability
of death. But being dead, he cannot ignore it; he can only avoid coming to grips with it. Toward the end of the novel Martin sees a red
lobster with which he becomes identified. A sudden horror grips him
because lobsters are red only when boiled. Random thoughts race
through his mind: Is he dead? Is there someone else on the rock? Is he
mad? Soon he is struck by another realization: guano, the manure of
sea birds, is insoluble. If this is the case, it is impossible for "slimy
wetness" to exist.

Another series of clues artfully prepares the way for the final symbolic identification of Martin with a lobster. The lobster claws, to
which he is finally reduced, had been mentioned earlier when Martin
peered into a trench containing crab shells, dead weed, and "the claws
of a lobster." Martin also saw a lobster whose sight repelled him. It is
ironic that he should be repulsed by his closest counterpart in the animal world, a creature whose claws are always extended with pincing
movements. He is finally reduced to a pair of lobster claws, a fitting
transformation for one who seized everything he wanted in life, just as
in Dante it is fitting that the thieves change back and forth into rep-
tiles since they converted the possessions of others into their own.

Golding's technique has thus far been masterful. He has taken the
reader into an illusory experience made vivid by a wealth of sensory

detail. Nor does he abandon the reader at the most harrowing moment of the tale: the reader is right there in Martin's consciousness. Both learn at the same time that the survival has been an illusion. The rest of the novel, except for the final chapter, follows inexorably: Martin, now aware that he is not among the living, must react to his discovery.

After Martin had demonstrated his naming prowess by designating the various districts on Rockall, he is about to call three rocks the Teeth, but recoils at the thought. Martin, the human mouth that reveled in masticating others, is afraid to impart such a name to the rocks; doing so would force him to realize that they represent himself. He then tries to sleep but cannot. The horror that he is enclosed within teeth and the fear that Rockall is shaped along the contours of a mouth take hold of him. Since he cannot sleep because "sleep is where we touch what is best left unexamined" (91), he must stay alert to avoid facing the truth. He cannot admit to himself that *he* is Rockall, a petrified mass in a boundless sea, for such an admission would destroy the illusion of his glorious survival. Thus he chooses to play a mad scene and to parody dialogue from *King Lear*.

If fate is character, Martin's fate is inevitable; by blaspheming, he wills his own destruction. Golding has only to let the myth take over; since Martin is now playing Capaneus, it is only logical that he should confront the God he scorns; and that the God should appear as a seaman, the form in which Martin has hallucinated him, modeling the Deity on himself. As he approaches the climax, Golding dispels any doubt that this is merely a survival story. God's question and Martin's reply make this clear: "Have you had enough, Christopher?" . . . Enough of what? Surviving. Hanging on" (194–95).

Now the real death occurs. Thus, when the novel was published in the United States in 1957, it bore the title, *The Two Deaths of Christopher Martin,* which had a neat literalness about it but not Golding's sanction. When real death comes, nothing of Martin's is spared, not even his claws. For him, it is not the Miltonic red lightning (*Paradise Lost* 1. 175) that was reserved for the fallen angels. For Capanean blasphemers the lightning is black. Yet something of Martin must persist: his soul. Even the Deity cannot annihilate that. If one assumes that Martin is reduced to nothingness, the novel's premise is false. *Pincher Martin* requires the same suspension of disbelief as the *Inferno*; it requires the acceptance of a soul with a personality that is a metaphor of the person. That Golding wished the reader to think of two stages in Pincher's afterlife, the purgatory on Rockall being the first, is evident from his own interpretation of the novel:

> Christopher Hadley Martin had no belief in anything but the importance of his own life; no love, no God. Because he was created in the image of God, he had a freedom of choice which he used to centre the world on himself. He did not believe in purgatory and therefore when he died it was not presented to him in overtly theological terms. The greed for life which had been the mainspring of his nature, forced him to refuse the selfless act of dying. He continued to exist in a world composed of his own murderous nature. His drowned body lies rolling in the Atlantic but the ravenous ego invents a rock for him to endure on. It is the memory of an aching tooth. Ostensibly and rationally he is a survivor from a torpedoed destroyer: but deep down he knows the truth. He is not fighting for bodily survival but for his continuing identity in the face of what will smash it and sweep it away—the black lightning, the compassion of God. For Christopher, the Christ-bearer, has become Pincher Martin who is little but greed. Just to be Pincher is purgatory; to be Pincher for eternity is hell.[4]

Golding is taking liberties with traditional Christianity, which regards purgatory as a place of temporal punishment from which release is possible; once released, the soul sojourns to heaven. The opposite happens to Martin who is released from purgatory and into hell. There is no doubt that Golding wishes us to consider Rockall as purgatory and, more specifically, a Dantean purgatory; Dante's purgatory is a mountain situated on an island. The chief difference, however, is that Golding's purgatory is a stopping-off point to hell.

Since *Pincher Martin* abounds in inversion and irony, the blasting of Martin from purgatory into hell is in keeping with the tone. Yet Golding is being more than ironic; he is exploring one of the great Christian paradoxes: the interconnection between God's mercy and the existence of hell. Dante would have put Martin in hell, perhaps in the seventh circle with Capaneus, although his treachery is really a sin of malice, the willing of evil to another and therefore a far more serious sin than blasphemy. At any rate, Golding would argue that if God is all-merciful, He would give Martin a second chance both in life and, to extend the paradox, in that zone between time and eternity over which God alone presides and in which the novel transpires. Martin rejects that mercy ("I spit on your compassion"); he also rejects heaven ("I shit on your heaven!"). Thus Martin has willed his place in the hereafter, the only place where he would be happy: hell. Here Dante and Golding agree. In Dante, one chooses hell because of what one is. The sinners, in fact, are anxious to reach their appropriate circle. Martin would have been unhappy in purgatory since, ultimately, he would have been sufficiently purged to move on to heaven. Martin wills hell where would-be murderers, rapists, and blasphemers are happiest; for, as Dante notes in one of the most profound paradoxes in *The Divine Comedy* (*Inferno* 3.4–6), God created hell out of love for those who want it, and Martin was among those who did.

Chapter Five
The Awful Rainbow
Mixing Memory with Desire

If one can imagine Christopher Martin with the capacity for salvation, he would be Sammy Mountjoy, the narrator of *Free Fall* (1959). Like Martin, Sammy relives incidents from his life; however, unlike Martin, Sammy is alive and voluntarily engages in memory therapy. By conjuring up fragments of his past, Sammy tries to give some direction to his amorphous present. In such self-analysis, detail is of the utmost importance; no memory is left untouched, no incident dismissed. Smells, moods, colors assume major significance when one is retracing the steps that led to spiritual malaise. Sammy seeks an answer to an overwhelming question: "When did I lose my freedom?"[1] After each remembered episode, he asks, "Here?" The reply, until the end of chapter 12, is always negative.

His earliest recollections are of his childhood in a Kentish slum, Rotten Row. Plagued by his illegitimacy, he finds little consolation in the conflicting versions of his whorish but good-natured mother. Since he is the typical fatherless boy, his first recollections are naturally of the female: Maggie, whom he sees while playing with a matchbox in the gutter; Evie, who fashions her own world of make-believe and revels in thoughts of urination; and Minnie, who relieves herself in the classroom with a complete lack of inhibition. In themselves these experiences are ordinary, yet they repeat themselves, as many of his childhood relationships do, in later life.

As Sammy matures and begins to move out of the world of Rotten Row, he exchanges his two main female influences, Ma and Evie, for males—Philip and Johnny. His actions become characteristically boyish—a nighttime excursion to an airport, trespassing on a general's estate, bullying younger boys. Again, none of these is particularly significant, and at the end of the first memory scene Sammy still has not found the moment he has been seeking: "No. Not here" (52).

In the second memory scene, Philip dares him to urinate on an altar, but Sammy is only able to spit. He is caught by Father Watts-Watt, the first in a series of Golding's homosexual stereotypes, who adopts Sammy after his mother's death. As Sammy closes this phase of his youth, he asks, "Well. There?" (70). The answer is negative.

The next recollection explores Sammy's first encounter with Beatrice. Now nineteen, an art student, and a Communist, he has had his first sexual experience and expects Beatrice to provide him with more. When he discovers she is frigid, he abandons her. Again the moment eludes him: "No. Not here" (132).

World War II and imprisonment in a concentration camp fail to supply the answer to the recurrent rhetorical question. Finally, Sammy recalls the words of his headmaster on graduation day: "If you want something enough, you can always get it provided you are willing to make the appropriate sacrifice" (235). Sammy wanted Beatrice and was willing to sacrifice everything to possess her. "Here?" he wonders. The question is never answered because it is foolish to belabor the obvious. Beatrice, who found her introduction to sex comparable to an innoculation, ends her days in a mental hospital, babbling incoherently and urinating with infantile abandon.

Although the critical reception accorded *Free Fall* was lukewarm, it did not diminish Golding's stature. Subsequently the novel found a few admirers;[2] when Golding won the Nobel Prize for literature, Anatole Broyard, the distinguished *New York Times* book critic, quoted the opening of *Free Fall* as an example of Golding's art—an art that obviously led to his winning the prize.[3] The rest of the novel, however, never quite delivers what the first page promises. First, there is something shopworn about the technique; one sees too clearly what the author is doing. Golding surrounds Sammy with pairs: Ma and Evie yield to Johnny and Philip, who in turn merge into Alsopp and Wimbury, his comrades in the Party. Beatrice and Taffy satisfy his sexual needs. His secondary school influences are also dominated by two extremes: Nick Shales, the atheistic scientist, and Miss Pringle, the neurotic religion teacher. The characters align themselves in pairs not because destiny has ordained it but because Golding has.

In one instance, Golding is successful in linking Sammy's past with his present. After the war Sammy learns that Beatrice has been institutionalized, and he visits her at the mental hospital. Chapter 13 links two seemingly unrelated episodes: Minnie's spontaneous urination in the classroom and Beatrice's fear of madness. Her fear has become a reality, and her psychosis has reduced her to gibberish ("Hi-yip!") and incontinence. Here Golding reveals the art of concealing art by bringing the past around full circle to impinge ironically on the present. Had the earlier part of *Free Fall* been constructed along such lines, the plotting would have been less transparent. The scaffold that was so magnificently dispensable in *Pincher Martin* has become all too visible in *Free Fall*.

Furthermore, there are two vital episodes—the interrogation by Dr. Halde and the ending—that lack conviction: the former because it is hackneyed, the latter because it is anticlimactic. Because Sammy knew of a planned escape from a concentration camp, he is brought before Dr. Halde, a Nazi psychologist, for cross-examination.

Halde understands Sammy completely; he knows that Sammy is an artist but an uncommitted one. Halde has also accurately gauged Sammy's breaking point. If one feels a certain familiarity about Dr. Halde, it is because he has appeared before in countless disguises as the articulate, dispassionate Nazi in World War II movies—the kind usually played by Erich von Stroheim, who abhors his present occupation but rationalizes it as expedient. Thus the confrontation between Sammy and Halde, which could have been a chilling confrontation between apathy and evil, dissipates into a melodramatic interrogation familiar to all movie fans, even to the point of including the inevitable "bloody swine!"

Sammy is incarcerated and subjected to mental torture. He is in complete darkness except for a piece of cold flesh that lies obscenely on the prison floor. The nature of the flesh is never specified, but it may well have been genital and intended to prey on Sammy's fear of castration.[4] In the prison sequence Golding momentarily recoups his art, describing Sammy's mental anguish with the same care that he lavished on Pincher Martin's ebbing consciousness. But the art wanes in chapter 8. Its opening question "How did I come to be so frightened of the dark? " begins forging links between present and past. Sammy's fears began after his mother's death and his adoption by Father Watts-Watt, whose pitiful advances occasion a digression on misdirected affection. As a child, Sammy fought imaginary enemies in the dark; now he contends with real ones in prison.

It is clear from the beginning of chapter 10 that Sammy was finally released; the rest of the novel concerns his postwar activities. But the ending is a return to the prison. The door opens, and a sympathetic officer apologizes for the treatment Sammy has received from Dr. Halde: "The Herr Doctor does not know about peoples." If this, the novel's last line, is supposed to throw the meaning of *Free Fall* into high relief, it does little more than to restate the obvious. The officer's words, while grammatically incorrect, reveal Dr. Halde's totalitarian conception of people: he may know the individual with clinical perception, but he is woefully ignorant of humanity. Yet this insight is gratuitous after the interrogation episode that establishes the type of person Halde is.

If Sammy's last recollection is of mercy offered ungrammatically, it is anticlimactic; if it is of a beneficent Nazi, the novel ends optimistically (for Sammy and humanity) with the conclusion that there were some good Nazis even in concentration camps. Since the arrangement of the incidents in Sammy's life has Golding's sanction, the final recollection must coincide with the author's intentions. But the ending follows the most significant episode in the novel—Sammy's visit to his "spiritual parents," Nick Shales and Rowena Pringle. Beforehand he prepared set speeches for each. He planned to explain Nick's atheism as the result of a primitive view of God. He would show Miss Pringle the fruit of her warped conception of religion—himself. Yet he would offer forgiveness, hoping to receive it in turn. As it happens, Sammy finds Nick dying in a hospital; Miss Pringle is so overjoyed to see her former student that she hopes she was in some way responsible for his success as an artist.

Both Nick and Miss Pringle represent extremes of which Sammy is aware: "Her world was real, both worlds are real. There is no bridge" (253). Humanity, then, is in a state of free fall, suspended between a humanism without God and a religion without humans. Golding is again working from a polarity—religion versus science. It would be futile to expect him to resolve the dilemma, especially since it seems to be a preoccupation.

Spanning the Bridge

There is no doubt that *Free Fall* is a personal and a quasi-autobiographical novel in which Golding transferred his prewar malaise to Sammy's postwar aimlessness and debated the possibility of bridging the chasm between the two forces that competed for Sammy's talents— science and the humanities. In the end, Golding felt, it was a gap that only the individual has the power to span. In 1961, two years after *Free Fall* appeared, Golding wrote: "Any man who claims to have found a bridge between the world of the physical sciences and the world of the spirit is sure of a hearing. Is this not because most of us have an unexpressed faith that the bridge exists, even if we have not the wit to discover it? "[5]

The same year he published an essay in *Holiday* magazine in which he recalled former teachers and school experiences.[6] The piece was not included in either collection of Golding's essays, perhaps because the author found it too self-revealing. When Golding was at Oxford studying the sciences but drawn to literature, he saw Albert Einstein standing on a bridge in Magdalen Deer Park. Neither could speak the other's language. Einstein pointed to a trout and said, "Fisch." Golding answered, "Fish. Ja. Ja." At that moment he would have sacrificed every bit of knowledge he had for an ability to speak German.

One expects a future writer to be more awed by a man of letters than by a scientist, and the respect that Golding evidenced for Einstein is touching. Golding never stopped hearing the siren call of science; it is not surprising that the echo reverberates in his reminiscences.

A Dark Wood

Free Fall begins with an interesting but (unfortunately) undeveloped premise: a man in his early thirties attempts to review his past life to see when he fell from grace. A parallel with Dante immediately suggests itself and, for a while, one thinks Golding will develop the premise along Dantean lines. Dante first saw Beatrice dressed in red, the patrician color, when both were nine. Sammy meets his Beatrice when their bicycles come to a halt at a red light; both are nineteen. While Dante's Beatrice was the ordering center of his cosmos, Sammy's Beatrice is an instrument for satisfying his lust. Sammy's surname is Mountjoy, a transparent double entendre if ever there was one. He is Sammy *Mons Veneris* ("Mount of Pleasure") and, appropriately enough, lives on Paradise Hill. For Sammy, Paradise and the Mount of Pleasure are synonymous; the *Mons Veneris* is the quintessential paradise.

Had Golding extended the Dantean parallels, *Free Fall* might have been a major mythic novel. Myth is Golding's metier; the memories and spiritual quest of a post–World War II wastelander cry out for mythopoesis—for a descent into a living hell or into the nightmare of history. Instead, Golding has taken a character whose existence is patternless and has imposed patterns on him.

Although Sammy is the narrator, Golding's omniscient voice does not quite synchronize with his protagonist's; in fact, it is often a bit louder than it should be. It is almost as if Golding were saying, "Here is a man without any moral direction but whose past is one vast web of connections with the threads carefully aligned in groups of two and producing a configuration of ordered anomie." Perhaps the patterns in Sammy's life are really an ironic commentary on his amorphousness; if so, any literary incongruity can be justified as irony.

The striking ordinariness of Sammy's life does not justify the amount of time and attention lavished on it. Furthermore, when Nick Shales and Rowena Pringle are introduced in chapter 12, the painstaking autobiography and the search for the lost moment of freedom are eclipsed by a third theme, the two cultures. It appears out of nowhere and dominates the chapter. This, one feels, is the novel's crux and has little to do either with Sammy's childhood in Rotten Row or his violation of Beatrice; it has to do with Sammy's inability to bridge the worlds of science and humanism. That inability is part of an eternal debate that had its origin in antiquity with the *nomos-physis* controversy and has continued in such forms as the "two cultures" theory. It is also a question that Golding himself has pondered. Golding is acutely aware of what C. P. Snow calls the "gulf of mutual incomprehension" that separates the scientist from the humanist, causing each to dislike and distrust the other.

Sammy's dilemma is Golding's. Even when Golding was at Oxford and growing disenchanted with science, he still had an appreciation, if not for the subject, then for what it could accomplish. He admits that "'science' is not the most important thing. Philosophy is more important . . . so is history."[7] Yet after *The Spire* (1964), which closed out the classical phase of his career, he confessed, "Now I must get in some sort of touch with the contemporary scene, and not necessarily the literary one; the scientific one perhaps."[8]

Clearly Golding wanted to reinterpret the conflict between science and humanism in terms of the Apollonian versus the Dionysian; he would have been on firm ground since Nietzsche in *The Birth of Tragedy* classifies science as Apollonian because it is based on the optimistic notion that answers can be found. But, unfortunately, like his protagonist-narrator, Golding became immersed in a sea of reminiscence.

An Unwitting Existentialist

One wishes Golding had cast *Free Fall* in a mythic mold, filling in the Dantean outline that was implicit from the beginning. The Dantean parallels, however, go nowhere; they only call attention to what might have been. Part of the problem lies in Golding's conflation of hell and purgatory, which were separate in *Pincher Martin,* but here merge into a metaphor for the contemporary world and Sammy's condition, which is a reflection of that world. The conflation occurs in the opening paragraph. Although admired as poetic prose (the narrator, a "burning amateur," feels "the flake of fire fall, miraculous and pentecostal" and sees dog-eared books "burst with a white hosanna"), it promises a world that never materializes. Golding cannot sustain the poetic intensity of a paradise that is really a purgatorial hell (or an infernal purgatory) because he cannot sustain the image. And yet, one wonders, if any modern writer could, except perhaps Thomas Pynchon, who managed to blend heaven, hell, and purgatory in *V.* and *Gravity's Rainbow.* In *Free Fall* the three states are not even a parodistic triad, only a brilliant but undeveloped idea, an embryonic metaphor.

Another problem with *Free Fall* is its unintended existentialism. Sammy is haunted by the loss of his freedom. He claims that, as a child, he was free; when confronted by two paths, he was able to take whichever he wanted. He was almost, but not entirely free, when he first saw Beatrice Ifor. To some extent, Golding is equating freedom with innocence, arguing that innocence is lost when the mind has its first glimpse into evil (Ralph, Lok). But innocence is a poetic construct like Arcadia or the Golden Age; one should really speak of the "myth of the loss of innocence" since it is difficult to find the precise point in time when it vanishes. Unable to recall our childhood innocence, we tend to idealize it.

If freedom and innocence are interlinked, to be free is to be able to choose; and true choice is the prerogative of the child. To a child, everything has its own special quality. Odors are particular ones, and each experience is unique. Thus Golding can speak of freedom as something to be tasted, like potatoes—a comparison that he repeats and that, apparently, has special meaning for him.

To understand what Golding means by freedom is to accept a paradox. Children may be free, but they really cannot lose freedom because they are innocent. As they mature and pass from innocence to experience, their freedom of choice is inevitably hampered by knowledge. Choice is not quite so simple as which path to take in a park.

To Golding, freedom is lost when individuals subordinate another person to their desires, reducing that person to an object of gratification. On his graduation day Sammy asked himself, "What is important to you?" The answer was Beatrice; to possess her, he agrees to sacrifice "everything." There is no longer any choice because he allows himself no alternatives; and if there is no choice, there is no freedom.

Freedom is a central issue in existentialist literature. Although Golding has pleaded ignorance of existentialism, he unwittingly ended up writing an existential novel—or rather, a parody of one. Freedom, which plagues Sammy, is also an existentialist obsession. In fact, Golding's concept of freedom, with its basis in choice and responsibility, has affinities with the existentialist *liberté*, in particular the idea that to be free, and therefore to be free to act, one must extricate the self from the morass of being-for-itself and aspire to being-for-others.

An existentialist would find Sammy in bad faith (*mauvaise foi*). He is uncommitted (*dégagé*); even art has not freed him to perform meaningful acts. Sammy bears a resemblance to Roquentin in Sartre's *Nausea*: both are trying to make sense out of the present; both are preoccupied with memories and sensations. Roquentin, however, is on the verge of becoming a true existentialist at the end of *Nausea*, relinquishing the past and plunging into the present which, for all its messiness, absurdity, and contingency, is all there is. Golding is too much of a Christian to have Sammy renounce the past, which is tantamount to renouncing history, and ultimately to renouncing God. To accept the present as the only reality is to be a Pincher Martin, who wanted being, pure being. The price was solipsism; the punishment, damnation.

Sammy is redeemable; while he seems to be heading down an existentialist path, Golding saves him from the black lightning by intervening as deus ex machina and enabling Sammy to pinpoint the moment he fell from grace, thereby providing a resolution to the novel, if not a solution to the problem. The problem can only be resolved by a Sartrean rejection of the past or by Dostoevskian suffering and redemption through love. Golding chooses neither.

Perhaps the real reason for *Free Fall*'s failure is the setting. Golding has never been at home in the contemporary world; except for *Darkness Visible*, which is not without flaws, he has never been successful at depicting it. His best work is set in the past, in the future, or in eternity.

Chapter Six

The Unsearchable Dispose

A Modern Classicism

It was inevitable that the blueprint for tragedy that Golding had been tracing in his first four novels would culminate in a work that was thoroughly informed by the tragic spirit; a work that charted the rise and fall of a protagonist cast between the extremes of virtue and vice but who pursues one goal exclusively. The protagonist of *The Spire* (1964) is Jocelin, Dean of the Cathedral of the Virgin Mary, who is obsessed with the goal of capping his church with a spire. Although his master builder warns him that the foundations cannot support the weight, Jocelin pays no heed and proceeds with a plan that brings death, madness, but ultimately triumph: as Jocelin lies dying, the spire still stands.

The Spire is not only as close a reproduction of classical tragedy as a contemporary author is likely to achieve; it is also as clear an example of mythmaking as students of literature are likely to find. Golding's classical allegiance makes his art difficult to define because, like that of the Greek tragedians, it achieves an artistic balance between opposites. Golding's case is complicated by the fact that the opposites not only include the primitive and the modern but also the pagan and the Christian. Even so, Golding is still very close to the Greek playwrights who worked with myths reflecting a barbarous past; myths of blood guilt, cannibalism, infanticide, parricide, matricide. The Greeks imposed artistic form on myth so that it became drama. Art tempered myth; it did not destroy it. The violence is still there, but it has been purified by poetry.

Sophocles' *Oedipus the King* is probably the best example of the transformation of myth into art. In its original, unpoetic state, the myth of Oedipus, involving as it does parricide and incest, would have seemed crude to Sophocles' fifth century B.C. audience. Likewise, Sophocles' irony, particularly such devices as the violent punning of *oida* ("I know") with the hero's name, would have been alien, if not unintelligible, to Greeks of an earlier period. The process, then, required the assimilation of myth into dramatic form, just as later *fabliau* was transformed into tale and chronicle into tragedy. The myth supplied the plot; the form purged the myth of those elements (inconsistency, lack of causality) that would otherwise anchor it to dream-narrative.

Although mythmakers are dependent on the past, that dependence does not make them unoriginal. Golding's novels are indeed derivative in the sense that they are parodies (in the author's special use of the word) of other works and myths. Nevertheless, drawing on the past is really a classical (or traditional, to T. S. Eliot's way of thinking) tendency. The classical artist was expected to conform to tradition. One way of conforming is to adhere to the boundaries staked out by one's predecessors—in itself, a form of acknowledgment. Another, better way to show one's gratitude to past authors is through allusions, reworked lines, and echoes. The ultimate goal is the assimilation of the past into the present.

In *Free Fall,* the assimilation is incomplete because the Dantean elements are primarily decorative. In *The Spire,* however, the assimilation is total; Golding works as a historical novelist would, transmuting sources into narrative so that the reader is completely unaware of the research. *The Spire* is, among other things, a historical novel; Golding is drawing on early English history—the construction of the spire of the Salisbury Cathedral in the fourteenth century.

In the Shadow of the Spire

Golding has spent most of his life in and around Salisbury, the site of the Cathedral Church of the Blessed Virgin Mary, whose great spire is visible from every point in the city as it pinions the sky in an act of self-transcendence. Ten miles to the north is Stonehenge, sown with relics of the past including a temple dating from around 1800 B.C.; thirty-five miles away is Avebury and a much larger ancient sanctuary. Wiltshire and the district around Salisbury, an area Golding knows intimately and loves passionately, illustrate the coalescence of paganism and Christianity but not the absorption of the former by the latter. There is tension in the landscape. Although Christianity triumphed, it could no more tame the wild and windswept plains of Salisbury than the Greek dramatists could purge myth of its violent passions. Despite the prominence of the cathedral, there is still something defiantly unbaptized about the hills around Salisbury.

Like its setting, *The Spire* is filled with a tension between the primitive past and the supposedly redeemed present. Even the workmen reflect that tension; they commit murder within the cathedral whose spire they are erecting. Christianity has failed to satisfy their darker needs; hence they still celebrate Midsummer's Eve and offer a human sacrifice to the gods of the foundations.

"There is no innocent work," Golding insists in the novel. Constructing a spire in the Middle Ages involved death and violence. Golding is not arguing that the end justifies the means, but rather that the means must be known if the end is to be understood. Thus Golding, moralist and mythmaker, historian and novelist, supports his thesis with facts. Certainly much of what is described in the novel can be corroborated. Jocelin's spire was to have a height of four hundred feet, approximately that of Salisbury's. Both spires are octagonal in shape; neither was constructed without rebellion, dissension, and a general indifference to liturgical forms—how else could construction progress unless services were curtailed or suspended? In 1762, when the capstone of the spire was undergoing repair, a small leaden box containing a relic of the Virgin Mary was discovered in a cavity.[1] In *The Spire,* Jocelin performs one last desperate act of faith by driving a Holy Nail, which has come from Rome, into the very point of the spire.

In an essay Golding retells the legend of the cathedral:

Round about the year 1200, Bishop Poore was standing on a hill overlooking the confluence of the local rivers, according to legend, when the mother of Jesus appeared to him, told him to shoot an arrow and build her a church where the arrow fell. The arrow . . . fell in the middle of a swamp. There, with complete indifference to such things as health, foundations, access and general practicability, the cathedral was built. Eighty years later . . . the builders erected the highest spire in the country on top of it, thousands of tons of lead and iron and wood and stone. Yet the whole building still stands. It totters. It bends. But it still stands.[2]

Just as Bishop Poore's instructions came from an apparition, Jocelin's inspiration comes from a vision. Furthermore, both Richard Fairleigh, the actual architect of the Salisbury spire, and Roger Mason, the master builder of the novel, went ahead with the construction even though they doubted the foundations would hold. Since Salisbury itself is built on marsh land, the Salisbury spire is said to have been "built on faith." In this instance, nature cooperated with faith; as it turned out, below the marsh was a stratum that was able to bear the load.

Still, in the thirteenth century, erecting such a spire would have been an act of folly. Thus Jocelin, whose name in Anglo-Saxon means "fool," is indeed a fool—if not for Christ's sake, then for God's.

Here the parallels end. A mythic or a historical novel can accommodate only so much background; then the writer's imagination comes into play. It is evident that the spire in Golding's novel is the Salisbury spire; however, the events leading to its construction and their configuration (or what Aristotle would call the *mythos*) are Golding's. The author who lived and even taught in its shadow saw the spire not as an architectural fact but as a symbol of faith, proceeding from an uncertain foundation but finally rising heavenward. Yet the erection of the spire poses some difficult questions: Does it warrant the sacrifice of four people? Is Jocelin right in ignoring murder and depravity in his cathedral so that his dream can be achieved? How can something be designed for God's glory when it threatens human life? The germs of tragedy latent in the story of the Salisbury spire might have eluded the literal eye of a chronicler, but they captured the imagination of Golding. The events obviously never happened as Golding describes them; but in art things happen as they *should* happen. As Aristotle noted in the *Poetics*, history depicts the particular; tragedy, the universal.

The Spire as Greek Tragedy

At the heart of the tragic process is a tension between two forces: the primitive and the civilized, the irrational and the rational. The same tension is inherent in myth itself, as Lillian Feder has argued with uncommon clarity in her definition of myth: "Myth is a narrative structure of two basic areas of unconscious experience which are, of course, related. First it expresses instinctual drives and the repressed wishes, fears, and conflicts that they motivate. These appear in the themes of myth. Second, myth also conveys the remnants within the individual consciousness of the early stage of phylogenetic development in which myths were created. This characteristic is evident mainly in its plots."[3]

The myths on which the Greeks based their dreams illustrate the tension between racial memory and liberated consciousness—a tension that, when dramatized, becomes a perennial conflict of opposites: the rationalism of Oedipus pitted against the mysticism of Teiresias, Medea's barbarism clashing with Jason's sophistry, Antigone's moral law challenged by Creon's man-made edict, the repressed Pentheus confronting the emancipated Bacchants. As the spiritual heir of the Greeks, Golding has inherited their traditions and their tensions.

The Spire works very much like a Greek tragedy in the sense that the tension or polarity determines the structure. The central conflict—Jocelin's supposedly noble vision to glorify the cathedral despite the dark forces within him that seek expression in the erection of the spire—is the axis on which the narrative rotates. That the construction will involve glory, suffering, and sacrifice is implicit in the opening paragraph: "He was laughing, chin up, and shaking his head. God the Father was exploding in his face with a glory of sunlight through painted glass, a glory that moved with his movements to consume and exalt Abraham and Isaac and then God again. The tears of laughter in his eyes made additional spokes and wheels and rainbows."[4]

Someone will have to be sacrificed for this vision; someone—or several persons, as it happens—will play Isaac to Jocelin's Abraham. Nor will God intervene to save the victim. There will be no confusion of heaven, hell, and purgatory as there was at the beginning of *Free Fall*. Back in a universe that he understands, Golding is able to generate ideas from images; in this case, three ideas derive from a single image of the sacrifice of Isaac on a stained glass window that is illuminated with sunlight as if the sacrifice had divine approval.

Glory and sacrifice are not mutually exclusive. Immediately after this explosion of light, the shafts of sun prove deceptive: they are not pure gold. The light is speckled with dust from the construction. Jocelin's motives, then, are not pure. But nothing is: *"There is no innocent work."* The spire is as much a reflection of Jocelin as it is a glorification of God.

Golding originally planned to call the novel *An Erection in Barcester*; fortunately, discretion prevailed. That the spire is Jocelin's dream erection is not only obvious; it also restricts the metaphor to one of sexual frustration, which is only one of several interrelated themes. The spire may be phallic, but there is something more unsettling about it. Jocelin pictures his church as a man lying on his back—arms outstretched in a Christus pose, with the spire projecting from his heart: "The model was like a man lying on his back. The nave was his legs placed together, the transepts on either side were his arms outspread. The choir was his body; and the Lady Chapel . . . was his head. And now also, springing, projecting, bursting, erupting from the heart of the building, there was its crown and majesty, the new spire" (4).

The disproportion in the model points to an imbalance in the maker.

The spire should exist as the crowning glory of a cathedral; instead, in Jocelin's vision it is the part that overshadows the whole. Jocelin is guilty of excess, always the contributing factor in the tragic hero's downfall. But before Golding relegates Jocelin to the charnel house of tragedy, he forces the reader to reconsider Jocelin's model. Architecturally, the model lacks proportion, yet conceptually it is valid. The cathedral, both in the novel and at Salisbury, is cruciform. Whether one compares it to a cross or to a crucified man is irrelevant. The "body" of the cathedral extends lengthwise from the west door to the Lady Chapel; the "arms," from the north to the south transepts with four pillars supporting the roof at the crossways.

The image, then, is one of concentric crucifixion—a crossway within a cross. Golding rarely works with a monovalent image; this one bourgeons like the apple tree in Jocelin's vision. If the interior of the cathedral is cruciform, crucifixion is inevitable—but with a twist: just as the hunter was the hunted in *Lord of the Flies,* the crucifier is the crucified in *The Spire.* Jocelin, who subordinates everyone to the spire, measuring their worth by what they can contribute to it, becomes the crucifier of two couples symbolized by the four pillars.

The Marriage of Hell and Heaven

The first couple is the verger Pangall and his wife Goody, whose baptismal name is never given; she is just a "Mrs.," unworthy of a given name because Jocelin does not think of her as a total person, but as a shock of red hair. The second couple is the master builder, Roger Mason, and his wife Rachel. Of the two couples, only Roger and Rachel are alive at the end. Actually, Roger is more dead than alive; an unsuccessful suicide attempt has left him mad. Jocelin fares no better; the crucifier is now the crucified. His spine wasted away by tuberculosis, Jocelin dies in the same supine position as his model.

Just as there is no innocent work, there is no one interpretation of *The Spire.* Golding's meanings are multilayered; his polyvalence is especially evident in his handling of the marriage theme. Since Jocelin's vocation precludes his marrying, he finds an outlet in the spire, "so that now there was a kind of necessary marriage: Jocelin and the spire" (88). But the spire is only a means of diverting his sexual energy (of which there seems to be an abundance) for something—or someone—else, namely, Goody Pangall, who continually excites him. Her red hair activates his satanic side—red being the satanic color. Although Jocelin is Goody's confessor and would like to consider her his daughter in God, the pull of the flesh is too strong.

Golding, the consummate ironist, does not leave it at that. Goody shares Jocelin's frustration; just as Jocelin's vows prevent him from consummating his love for her, Pangall's impotence prevents the consummation of their marriage. When Goody finds herself in the presence of a virile male like Roger, Jocelin, unable to possess Goody himself, begins to envision her and Roger as a couple, separated from the rest of the cathedral by wood and canvas. What Jocelin cannot have with Goody, Roger can—and with Jocelin's blessing. Although Jocelin is initially appalled at Roger's growing attraction to Goody, he knows the practical function she will serve: "She will keep him here" (59); and that, at a time when qualified masons are rare, is not to be dismissed.

As Jocelin's marriage to the spire becomes indissoluble, he changes markedly. First he is transfigured with joy, God the Father exploding in his face. But the euphoria does not last. Although he insists "the spire isn't everything," it becomes clear that it is. The vision swells into an obsession, altering everything that comes within its orbit. For construction to take place, religious services are suspended, and the high altar is barricaded. Devotion is impossible in the midst of scaffolds and in the presence of workmen later revealed to be little more than degenerates. When Pangall tells Jocelin there has been a murder, Jocelin's dispassionate reply is "I know"; when Pangall complains of being mistreated, Jocelin's answer is "You're too thin-skinned, man" (15). Jocelin has no more intention of alienating the workers than he does of losing Roger's services. Jocelin is quite capable of averting his gaze, even to the point of ignoring the workers' paganism, which Christianity has been unable to change. In some ways, Jocelin's behavior recalls Piggy's. After Simon's murder, Piggy insists it was an accident rather than admit the truth. Jocelin does virtually the same when the workers kill Pangall, who, like Simon, is a sacrifice to the dark gods—specifically, to the cthonic deities in the foundations they believe might be appeased by a human offering.

In Golding, just as one meaning spawns another, one paradox generates a series. A helllike pit gapes at the crossways; while the pit is necessary for construction, the workers use it as the equivalent of the ancient cornfields where the Year Kings were buried in the expectation that their corpses would fertilize the soil. From another point of view, the pit is hell-on-earth, located in the least infernal of places, in a cathedral.

The spire must go down as far as it goes up. Descent, then, is the prerequisite for ascent; in mythic terms, descending to the underworld is preliminary to assuming a role in revitalizing society or, in the case of Aeneas, to founding a city. In *The Spire,* the characters must go through hell before they can be judged worthy of heaven, or at least of salvation. Once their ordeal is over, once the spire has been raised, the pit will cease to exist. But until then, the old order prevails; the end—the glory of God—justifies the means, the inglorious manipulation of humankind: "If they are part of the cost, why so be it" (95). Thus Jocelin deceives a competitor, causing Roger to lose a better offer. People are reduced to physical features or to subservient forms of life. Just as Goody becomes an erotic object, synecdochally reduced to her blazing hair, Roger becomes a prey, an animal in Jocelin's "open trap," a "prisoner for this duty," a "slave for the work." And Jocelin becomes God's hunter as well as His fool.

Classical/Christian, Conscious/Unconscious

Since *The Spire* is an alloy of the classical and the Christian, Golding shifts back and forth between them, using motifs first of one and then of the other. Jocelin has his own pagan substratum, his Dionysian cellarage, on which he has built his priesthood. Thus he sometimes behaves like a classical protagonist, so obsessed with his vision that he refuses to heed the warnings of nature. He ignores a series of prodigies—the inexplicable crying of children, the eerie singing of the cathedral pillars, a plague rumor, an earth tremor, and a raven that flies past him on three separate occasions. The final proof that the spire has become a personal undertaking occurs when Jocelin affixes his own seal to a document approving additional building costs.

There are times when Jocelin behaves like a myth-haunted figure, able to see the world only through the gauze of the collective unconscious. Then the action grows ambiguous, and the narrative halting; yet Golding never loses control. *The Spire* is a perfect example of what Wayne Booth calls a third-person narrator-agent novel; that is, a third-person novel whose central character exerts such an influence on the action that he or she seems to be telling the story. *The Spire* has the air of a confession, with the central consciousness split into psyche and ego, each recording and reacting in its own way. When situations arise that are too painful for Jocelin or that are at variance with his priesthood, he responds like a dreamer who is aware that there is such a thing as the waking state but is unwilling to accept it. Thus incidents such as the budding romance between Goody and Roger, Goody's pregnancy, and Rachel's description of her husband's suicide attempt have a suppressed, sublimated quality, as if they have been understood only on an unconscious level. Like everything in the novel, Jocelin is divided; part of him seeks self-transcendence through an act of faith; part yields to a sensuous reverie from the sight of red hair or the phallic model of a spire.

Jocelin is so neurotically circumspect about sex that whenever he feels the slightest physical urge, his unconscious takes over the narration, presenting the action metaphorically and imagistically, as if it were loath to be direct. At the end of chapter 6, Jocelin experiences a dream that is his punishment for manipulating Roger Mason. He imagines himself lying in a Christus pose on the marshes like the model of the cathedral. But instead of sun streaming through the windows, Satan appears naked with red hair, an androgynous amalgam of the devil and Goody. The sight causes him to writhe on the marsh in "warm water," Jocelin's euphemism for semen. That the dream ended in ejaculation is clear from Jocelin's reaction to it: he is filled with such self-loathing that he flagellates himself.

Yet there are times when Jocelin speaks with the confidence of one who realizes his position in the divine scheme of things. In his speech to Roger Mason, he is quite specific about the role he is playing in the execution of the divine will: "When such a work is ordained, it is put into the mind of a, of a man. That's a terrible thing. I'm only learning now, how terrible it is. It's a refiner's fire. . . . You and I were chosen to do this thing together. It's a great glory. I see now it'll destroy us of course. What are we, after all?" (83). And again: "You're not in my net. . . . It's His. We can neither of us avoid this work" (115).

The Tragic Process

The Spire not only recreates the spirit of classical tragedy; it also recreates the tragic process. Golding has taken Jocelin along the same course that Oedipus traversed, as a comparison between *The Spire* and Sophocles' *Oedipus the King* reveals. Both works exhibit the following:

The tension between conscious motivation and unconscious

desire. The spire, originally conceived as an adornment for a house of God, becomes a monument to frustrated sexuality and an indomitable will. Oedipus's conscious attempt to find the murderer of Laius runs parallel to, and ultimately coincides with, his unconscious attempt to uncover his origins. The erection of the spire and the investigation of the murder are both conscious endeavors and manifestations of the characters' unconscious.

Fusion of hero and mission.   Jocelin's relation to his vision is described as a "necessary marriage." Oedipus's mission is not much different: it is a merging of identities, of quester and quest. Immediately after Oedipus learns that the murderer must be expelled from Thebes, he begins his investigation, vowing to champion the dead king as if he were his own son. His identification with his cause grows until he discovers the murderer; however, the one he has been seeking is himself. Oedipus is the object of his own investigation.

Change in the personality of the king-figure.   As Jocelin's goal becomes an obsession, he changes from a priest to a visionary, subordinating and sacrificing everything and everyone to the spire. He turns the cathedral into a home for fornicators and sodomites, condones adultery, practices deception, tolerates murder, and is indirectly responsible for the deaths of two people and another's madness. Oedipus, who originally regarded himself as a father-king bound by cosmic sympathy to his children-subjects, evolves into a tyrant; hence the play's Greek title, *Oedipus Tyrannus*. His insistence on clarity becomes a nagging literalism. He taunts Teiresias, whose veiled language infuriates him; he even vents his wrath at Creon and finally at Jocasta, who, he suspects, is afraid the investigation will prove him illegitimate.

Tragic knowledge.   In *Oedipus the King,* the final stage in the tragic process is the protagonist's realization that he has accomplished his purpose, but with an ironic and unanticipated outcome: Oedipus has succeeded in finding Laius's murderer, and in doing so, has passed from ignorance to knowledge. But the knowledge Oedipus acquires is not merely factual; the facts themselves are part of the fabric of Oedipus's life. In learning about the past, he has learned about himself. He has reconstructed his own biography. Or rather, he has composed his autobiography, for in autobiography, subject and object coincide.

Jocelin's knowledge is more complex. He knows early in the novel that he is an executor of God's will. In itself this is not cosmic knowledge but orthodox Christianity, which teaches that the minister of the Gospel is a servant of Christ and a steward of God's mysteries (1 Cor.

4:2). The real knowledge Jocelin acquires is deathbed knowledge. To make certain that the reader understands the difference, Golding italicizes Jocelin's insights so that they stand apart from the narrative and are not confused with his visions or utterances. For these are Jocelin's final thoughts (not last words since they remain unspoken): *"How proud their hope of hell is. There is no innocent work. God knows where God may be. It's like the apple tree!"* (214–15).

There is something rhetorical about his first realization; "proud hope" is an oxymoron, a juxtaposition of two seeming opposites. Jocelin is making a universal statement about pride and hope, not about the proud and hopeful. Previously, he had imagined humankind wrapped in parchment. To a modern reader, the vision might seem curious, but not to a medieval priest who read from parchment. Humanity, then, is a book, a manuscript of pride, a readable text. If pride brings humans to hell (and as the deadliest of the seven deadly sins it should), the proud have willed it; if their being tends toward hell, they naturally hope to achieve it, just as the righteous hope to gain heaven. If pride is sinful, so is the hope of the proud; for them, hope is not a virtue but a vice.

Jocelin, however, is one of the proud. He is, in fact, so proud that when he overhears some deacons speaking about him, calling him proud and ignorant, he assumes they mean someone else. Yet Jocelin is proud and ignorant, although not one of the parchment people. Jocelin's pride is not "the never failing vice of fools" as Pope terms it in *An Essay on Criticism.* Jocelin may be a fool, but he is God's fool. Originally, he is swollen with self-importance, but he is deflated when he finds it was not his learning that made him dean of the cathedral but the whim of the king, whose mistress was Jocelin's aunt. The position was a plum that the king tossed to Jocelin at his aunt's urging.

Such a plum would naturally make a man like Jocelin proud. But his pride is not hybris; it is not arrogating to oneself what is God's. Jocelin knows he is "a, a man" but not "a learned man," as he himself admits. Unfortunately, Golding forgets that Jocelin could barely read the "Our Father" and, on his deathbed, has Jocelin utter the name of Berenice, who dedicated her hair to Ptolemy III. Jocelin is thinking, as he constantly does, of Goody's hair. Still, the allusion is inappropriate. The only way a medieval priest could have known of Berenice would have been through Catullus's poem, *The Lock of Berenice (Coma Berenices).* But familiarity with Catullus, much less with his most difficult poem, would have been impossible in the fourteenth century.

First, Catullus was not part of the medieval trivium; second, even if he were, Jocelin's Latin was so bad (he has trouble, after all, with the *Pater noster*) that he could have scarcely made it past the first line. Irony and allusion have pitfalls that Golding is generally able to avoid. While, in this instance, he falls into the trap of double irony, he manages to extricate himself, however implausibly, through Father Adam's response when he hears the name Berenice. "Saint?" Father Adam asks. To humor him, Jocelin answers, "Saint."

Jocelin's insights are like the movements of César Franck's Symphony in D Minor, in which despair struggles with hope—one winning, then the other—until reconciliation is achieved, neither being victorious. Thus Jocelin's vision of a proud race hoping for hell is tempered by a sobering insight into the ways of God: "*There is no innocent work.*" There is nothing that does not bring evil in its wake, even the *opus dei*, the work of God. What matters only is that the good outweigh the evil.

"*God knows where God may be.*" Even if "God knows" is interpreted as an expression of doubt ("God knows when we shall meet again"), the basic concept of an omniscient and immanent God remains: God is present everywhere and in everything, even in a man chosen to do His work despite a mind bursting with fantasies and a tuberculosis eating away his spine.

"*It's like the apple tree!*" is the coda, drawing together the strands of Jocelin's thought as well as crystallizing an earlier vision in which Jocelin sees the spire as something that began simply, like a single green shoot that first bourgeoned into tendrils and finally into branches. In this image, Jocelin sees the divine as well as the demonic, for among the leaves is a "long black thing," the serpent. To understand the full meaning of the serpent in the tree is to realize that even in Eden before the Fall, there was the possibility of a fall; and to separate the tree from the serpent is to misunderstand both God and humankind. Redemption has not driven the serpent from the tree, any more than baptism has eradicated original sin. To realize this is to accept humankind with all its greatness and limitations, and life in all its glory and horror. The spire, with its complementary and contradictory meanings, is humankind's dialectic. One meaning that can never be lost is the erotic, for the inspiration to glorify God can be as much the result of sexual as of spiritual energy. Jocelin's last thought of the spire is that it is "as slim as a girl," rising up to the sky with a "silent cry," never able to reveal what brought it to its height.

Despite the cost, the spire is still a work of art that reminds Jocelin of an upward flowing waterfall. That the last image is an inversion is not surprising; it is the inversion that resolves the others. The spire, while it came from the Fall, is not *of* the Fall; it does not look down, like the waterfall in *The Inheritors,* but upward. The spire is a symbol of hope, not for the proud, for theirs is the hope of hell; but for the humble, for whom it is an act of faith. To accept something as a product of the Fall but unable to fall is to understand the great paradox of human nature: humankind's ability to soar into infinity from the most finite of bases.

Chapter Seven

The Pharaohs of England

Building the Pyramid

Although Golding has written short fiction, it has never been his forte; his few short stories are preliminary sketches for his novels, or in the case of "Envoy Extraordinary" (1956), for a play, *The Brass Butterfly* (1958). The seeds of *Darkness Visible* (1979), in which a central character is facially disfigured, can be found in "The Anglo-Saxon" (1959) where a Briton finds himself in an oedipal situation: he encounters some American soldiers on a road and argues with them over the right of way.[1] After attacking one of them, he is hauled off to jail and fined five pounds. The fine is paid by the soldier the Briton assaulted: a black man whose scarred face is covered with bandages the same color as his skin.

The significance of "The Anglo-Saxon" does not lie in its literary merit, which is slight; the story is unsatisfying, arousing pathos but lacking conviction. In attempting to impart heroic dignity to a character whose 650-word vocabulary "hung like hooks" in a "dark cupboard," and who brandishes an ashplant in an act of tribal self-assertion, Golding has made the inarticulate Briton a brother to Ralph and Lok. While Ralph and Lok witness signs of humanity's scarred nature, the Briton beholds its scarred face. While the three of them weep in response to the human condition, Ralph and Lok at least have some inkling as to why they weep: for the darkness of the heart, for the end of the species. The Briton, on the contrary, "did not understand the hot tides that filled his eyes with water."

Although it is a failure as a short story, "The Anglo-Saxon" is important for another reason: it offers evidence of Golding's interest in contemporary life—an interest that began in the late 1950s, around the time he was writing *Free Fall*, his first contemporary novel. In 1960–61, he wrote two radio plays—*Miss Pulkinhorn* (1960), set in a cathedral town not unlike Salisbury; and *Break My Heart* (1961), about

78

a student in a British public school, written when the author was in his *Free Fall* frame of mind.[2]

Miss Pulkinhorn, a tale of muted violence with a surprise ending, is the precursor of *The Spire.* The narrator, later identified as Graham, the organist, establishes the mood in a voice familiar to all radio devotees: "Darkness in the cathedral. Gleams, no more, from gold and brass and silver. Puddles of half-light from bulbs swinging sometimes on twenty yards of flex. And the echo!"

Graham recounts his first experience with Miss Pulkinhorn, an implacable opponent of change, who criticizes his unorthodox selection of liturgical music. She is even more concerned about the disquieting presence of a man who interrupts the services with "hosannah" and whose only comfort comes from seeing the red tabernacle light that indicates the presence of the sacrament. Golding again establishes a polarity, here based on an ageless antagonism—a rigid orthodoxy that makes no allowance for the visionary, and a mysticism that cannot be subjected to church etiquette. Miss Pulkinhorn has appeared before in various guises: she is Ralph or Jack, depending upon whose star is in the ascendant in the eternal conflict; she is the modern age casting a dark shadow on an earthly paradise. Hers is the most deadly form of rationalism—the unproductive that manifests itself only in prejudice. The man is also a familiar Golding figure, one of a long line of Christ-figures who suffer intensely but silently, and whose names are enrolled in the author's litany of saints.

Miss Pulkinhorn knows that the man's sanity hinges on his belief that the sacrament is present in the tabernacle. Traditionally, the sanctuary candle is not lighted when the sacrament is not present. One evening, when the eucharist has been removed for the purpose of a sick call, Miss Pulkinhorn stealthily enters the cathedral and lights the candle. The man, who is late for his evening visitation because he has stopped to give his shirt to a beggar, enters to find the light burning but the tabernacle door ajar. He also finds Miss Pulkinhorn waiting for him in the dark with the news that the tabernacle is empty. The man dies of shock and despair, but Miss Pulkinhorn insists her conscience is clear. "A week later she was dead."

Miss Pulkinhorn was an engrossing radio play, but Golding made the mistake of adapting it as a short story.[3] Miss Pulkinhorn's revenge is so grotesque and personal that it can only be described after the fact, because it entails an action that she performs but that can only be known if she recounts it herself.

Exposition has never been Golding's forte; he is always at his best when he weaves fragments of biography in and out of the narrative (*Pincher Martin*) or presents his characters without formal introduction, expecting the reader to establish the necessary relationships (*The Inheritors*). One has no quarrel with voice-over narration in radio drama, where it has a long-standing tradition, or with first-person narration in fiction. But a narrator who must explain both the climax and the denouement of an action in which he did not even participate weakens the story, since his words have only the force of conjecture. From the moment Miss Pulkinhorn enters the cathedral, the revenge is completely her own. A switch to the third person would have been far more effective than the unwarranted appearance of a narrator. The gothic tale requires subtlety; one wishes Golding had studied Faulkner's "A Rose for Emily."

In his second radio play, *Break My Heart,* Golding casts a cold eye on another British tradition, the public school. The play is characteristic of Golding's technique. There is no formal introduction of the characters; they appear as if the listener had known them for years. The action begins with a number of seemingly disconnected scenes of public school life. At first little is in focus, except an inept faculty incapable of understanding students; gradually attention falls on Malcolm Smith, a student who cannot memorize Hamlet's "O that this too too solid flesh" soliloquy. The boy's mental block brings the drama to its climax. The construction of the events leading to it throws much light on Golding's art, especially his ability to build a scene by employing a full range of visual and aural effects.

In the final scene the aged Pennyfeather thinks of his students and absentmindedly recites their names: "Anderson, Fulbright, Noakes, Rogers, Pain, Smith. Smith—(pause). Why should I think of Smith? Why should I think of anyone? (yawning). Why should anyone think of anyone? Does he think of me? Does he think at all? I wonder what he's thinking now—" A sound cue calls for "WIND. HEART BEAT IN THE WIND." A group of boys chants derisively: "Smith-y, Smith-y, Smith-y, how's yer Ma Smith-y? How's yer Ma?" Smith is heard muttering in his sleep with the chanting in the background. The sound cue reads: "Chant continues but FADES INTO BACKGROUND. FOREGROUND, STUMBLING STEPS ON A CARPETED STAIR. GIGGLES."

Smith cannot memorize the soliloquy because it is too reminiscent of his own situation: like Gertrude in *Hamlet,* his mother is also involved in an adulterous relationship with her brother-in-law. In the ironic final scene, his teacher tries to explain the context: "You see, Hamlet feels that his mother is almost committing incest by letting her husband's brother make love to her." But then he adds: "At your age you can't understand a thing like this by the light of nature or through experience." Like Hamlet, Smith can only hold his tongue despite his breaking heart. *Break My Heart* reads like a discarded chapter from *Free Fall* with Malcolm Smith and his mother as upper-class reincarnations of Sammy Mountjoy and Ma.

"The Anglo-Saxon" and the radio plays were preliminary sketches of English village life that Golding planned to expand into a novel. One element, however, was lacking: a central character. Thus he attempted another sketch before taking on the monolith known as the British class system by reworking material from *Free Fall* and *Miss Pulkinhorn*. As "Inside a Pyramid" (1966) opens, Oliver, the narrator, returns to his home in the fictitious Stilbourne, where Miss Pulkinhorn lives and which is intended to evoke Marlborough where Golding attended grammar school. There he learns that his former violin teacher, Clara Cecilia Dawlish (affectionately called "Bounce"), is dead. The sight of her name on a tombstone occasions an extended reminiscence of his relationship with her. What begins as a man's recollection of an unforgettable character ends with a tortured farewell to a woman who was actually a loveless neurotic, totally lacking in the sensitivity that her profession required. Unlike Sammy Mountjoy of *Free Fall* who returned to his teacher Miss Pringle (an earlier version of "Bounce") with a message of forgiveness, Oliver can only stare at the tombstone and cry: "I never liked you. Never!"[4] Yet he cannot account for the grief that has come over him.

From the Escarpment to the Summit

When Golding's fifth novel, *The Pyramid,* was published in the fall of 1967, it was advertised as a "new novel," but "new" was hardly the right word. Readers of the *Kenyon Review* (June 1967) had already been prepared for it by a short story, "On the Escarpment," which was labeled "a section from Mr. Golding's forthcoming novel."[5] If *KR* subscribers were also devotees of *Esquire,* they might have recalled a similar Golding story in the December 1966 issue in which "Inside a Pyramid" appeared, enclosed between Christmas ads for Bulova watches and Bols liqueurs. Clearly the sides of *The Pyramid* had been constructed and were awaiting a base.

Instead of a base, however, Golding only added a new episode, imparting at best an artificial unity. Still, *The Pyramid* is neither the "embarrassment" it has been called[6] nor the verbal sonata that Golding has termed it.[7] It is an episodic work that lacks Golding's customary mosaic exactness. The sketches have become vignettes—three selected incidents in the life of the narrator Oliver, spanning a period from the early 1930s through 1963 and recorded without the customary chapter headings so that the flow of memories is not impeded. Had Golding exercised greater control over his own memories, much less those of his narrator, he might have produced a tighter narrative. It is obvious that when "Inside a Pyramid" was published, Golding had either written "On the Escarpment" or knew what it would contain. In "Pyramid," Oliver alludes to Evie, but the allusion is meaningless without a knowledge of "On the Escarpment." Whether she is the same Evie who urinated her way through the early chapters of *Free Fall* is irrelevant; the center does not hold because there is none. There is only a novel that began as two stories with a common narrator—"Inside a Pyramid" (1966) becoming the closing episode and "On the Escarpment" (1967) constituting the opening one.

The first page of *The Pyramid* promises a new Golding, or at least a return to the Golding of *Free Fall* without the postwar malaise. The writing has a youthful intensity and a suggestion of the bucolic; it is also considerably more conventional than anything the author had attempted heretofore: "It was really summer, but the rain had fallen all day and was still falling. The weather can best be described by saying it was the kind reserved for church fetes. The green leaves were being beaten off the trees by the steady downpour and were drifting about in the puddles."[8]

Clearly there was no loss of artistic integrity in the new Golding; the loss was one of vigor. The energy of Hellenism dissipated in the English countryside as Golding went from being a critic of humankind to a critic of society.

Social criticism is already present in *Free Fall,* the true precursor of *The Pyramid.* Sammy Mountjoy, the prototype of Oliver, is the product of a slum environment, a sluttish mother, an atheistic science teacher, a sexually repressed teacher of religion, and a frigid mistress. This compendium of neuroses is, of course, an oversimplification and to Golding's credit he never assumed the mantle of amateur psychologist to enumerate the reasons for Sammy's loss of freedom. Still, the detailed account of Sammy's youth in Rotten Row leads one to suspect that there is as much sociology as theology operating in the novel—a factor that may explain why it is so unsatisfying.

In *The Pyramid* Golding becomes a social mythmaker; he has progressed from a mythical universe (The Coral Island) through mythical heroes (Lok, Pincher Martin, Jocelin) to a mythical community with a name so transparent it requires no commentary—Stilbourne. A sleepy town in the South of England where the mask of respectability stifles an adolescent's outcry against class distinction, it is found in the county of Barchester (the setting of *The Spire,* courtesy of Trollope). Stilbourne is Sinclair Lewis's Gopher Prairie, Thomas Wolfe's Altamont, Sherwood Anderson's Winesburg, Ohio, and every hamlet where young talent suffocates, where boys who should be musicians are turned into scientists by pragmatic parents, and where girls from the lowest social stratum resort to prostitution. Golding's geography, while much less elaborate than Faulkner's Yoknapatawpha County, expresses a type of myth that is new to the author but not without literary precedent: the myth of the social monolith as illustrated by Stilbourne, Oliver the narrator, and Evie, "our local phenomenon."

Golding lavishes a great deal of care on the beginning of his books. Anyone who merely scans the first few pages will never penetrate the world of the novel. The opening of *Pincher Martin* describes a man at the moment of drowning with such sensory detail that one must accept the incident without as yet understanding its significancce. Readers who grow impatient with description will enter the novel after the introduction, moving from one memory maze to another and calling a carefully woven web of reminiscence a labyrinth of unintelligibility.

Golding demands that similar attention be paid to the opening of *The Pyramid.* Oliver is summoned by Evie, imploring him to help Bob Ewan who has driven Miss Dawlish's car into a pond. In a Golding novel, characters are introduced either in relation to a specific situation (*Lord of the Flies*) or an object (the log in *The Inheritors,* the spire). A car stuck in a pond is hardly worthy of attention except that the car belongs to Oliver's music teacher, to whom the third episode is devoted, and that in it were Evie and Bob, the local phenomenon and the local pride.

The three are victims of a society that allows the slut from Chandler's Close (Evie), the doctor's son (Bob) and the son of the local druggist (Oliver) to interact only in time of crisis and then only because of a social code that requires an inferior to aid his superior. Ewan sought Evie out partly because her aloofness intrigued him, but more so because sex was only possible with the proverbial girl from the other side of the tracks. Oliver grew up next door to the Ewans, literally in their shadow and always aware of the distinction between the son of a doctor and the son of a druggist.

Oliver must also possess Evie, but for more complex reasons. He is eighteen, and the woods are "hot" and "sexy." He also knows that Ewan had Evie first and that he was summoned to help them return a car that had been used for a night of lovemaking. Oliver's need for sexual fulfillment is aggravated when he finds Ewan's mud-caked trousers, which his imagination transforms into a love trophy.

There are obvious parallels with *Free Fall* and Sammy's deliberate conquest of Beatrice Ifor. Oliver's awakening to sex, typical of an eighteen-year-old virgin anxious to change his status, is complicated by other factors—his growing awareness of Stilbourne's vacuity, his social inferiority, his sweetheart's betrothal, and a professional interest in music that must yield to his parents' wishes.

The early part of the first episode is devoted to Oliver's planned seduction of Evie; the technique is masterful, although to many readers Oliver emerges from his dubious triumph a cad. "The scene" is more explicit than anything Golding has ever written, yet the author remains a would-be poet, describing female anatomy in terms of rose petals. It also answers the critics who have accused Golding of being indifferent to women. Evie is Golding's most realistic female, although she has appeared before in the works of others—as Bessie Watty in Emlyn Williams's *The Corn Is Green,* for instance. Evie is the typical slum girl abused by men, especially by Captain Wilmot, supposedly teaching her secretarial skills but really instructing her in masochism, as the welts on her body attest. Yet Evie is also the vengeful whore turned respectable mistress who accuses Oliver of raping her because she believes he has spread malicious gossip about her father and herself. Evie is complex, or as complex as a village prostitute can be; it is a tribute to Golding's humanity, a quality many critics would deny him, that he can write so compassionately about her.

Yet the first episode is Oliver's story, although, like most hero-narrators, he remains faceless. His lust crystallizes into an erotic vision that turns the forest into a sexually inviting woodland, Evie's eyes into plums, and her odor into a scent. His first attempt at sex culminates in onanism; his second, not much better, leaves him wondering whether Evie will get pregnant. Evie, the abused trollop, needs love desperately, but cannot give herself to Oliver. A budding intellectual torn between science and music, Oliver needs the same love and with the same intensity, but is incapable of conveying it. One is back again with Jack and Ralph, Sammy and Beatrice, Jocelin and his spire. Golding's loveless are so enmeshed in their own neuroses that when they attempt something human, they are not only incapable of basic tenderness but also fail at the most elementary expressions of it.

Oliver's sexual awakening arouses the poet in Golding, who first compares Evie's eyes and mouth to plums and then, as the eroticism becomes total, makes them plums:

Her face was very white, mouth and eyes like black plums (6).
The plums glanced up at me over her hands (6).
My mind's eye saw, not the wet and draggled Evie, her face reduced to three plums in a patch of white (97).
The only light came from Evie, her three black plums so close to me against the pier (36).
Three plums and a glimmering skin, vibration— (40).[9]

Golding used this technique before; when Pincher Martin calls part of Rockall "the Dwarf," it soon becomes a dwarf and assumes a dwarf-like role. This device in which the epithet unites with the object has a timelessness about it, perhaps because it was the way that poetry originated—from an essential oneness between the poet and the natural environment.

The first episode ends melodramatically, but not with the gimmickry of which Golding is often accused. Oliver meets Evie after an absence of two years. He had gone on to study science at Oxford, and she to join the kept women of London. In a Stilbourne pub, she accuses Oliver of raping her. The accusations carry over to the street where Evie rails at Oliver for "telling an' laughing." "What about?" asks Oliver. "Me 'n' Dad," she answers (90).

The outburst is sheer theatre, and Golding has never avoided the theatrical. The rage that Evie suppressed during her years in Stilbourne erupts in a denunciation of Oliver, who used her as selfishly as the others. Now it is clear why she insisted that Oliver take her on a hill outside Stilbourne where anyone with binoculars, including Oliver's father, could watch them make love. But Evie implied more than abuse; she accused Oliver of belittling her. Yet it was he who felt inferior to Bob Ewan. Or does "Me 'n' Dad" mean something else— something more psychological than social? Incest perhaps? One is never told, and Oliver returns home meditating on "her curious slip of the tongue."

The second episode, which had not been published before, could be entitled "Beyond the Escarpment." It satirizes Stilbourne's artistic aspirations. Oliver has returned from Oxford after his first term and is recruited into a production of *King of Hearts,* the type of operetta the bourgeoisie consider high art. Stilbourne is as committed to its superficial cultural life as it is to its artificial social structure. The operetta is a community enterprise with the usual rivalries and altercations that arise when amateurs fancy themselves professionals.

While Oliver is still the central figure in the second episode, he does not dominate it. Like Aeneas, he is always being eclipsed by characters more interesting than himself; perhaps that is the fate of a narrator-agent. Now it is the director, Evelyn de Tracy, who commands our interest, compassion, and ultimately, respect.

In his youthful quest for truth, Oliver seeks out the sophisticated Evelyn and poses the perennial question: where is the *"truth* of things?" When Evelyn shows him one form of truth, the truth of sexual maladjustment, which causes him to pose as a woman to the point of dressing up as a ballerina, Oliver bursts into laughter. He has never encountered a transvestite before, and his desire to continue the conversation with Evelyn is as much the result of youthful fascination with deviant behavior as the need to communicate with an educated person. When Evelyn finally disappears on the wrong bus, Oliver is left shouting his name exactly as he had called after the departing Evie at the end of the first episode.

There is, however, a difference in chronology: the second episode takes place before the first has ended. Oliver sees Evie for the last time shortly before he begins his third year at Oxford; the operetta is staged at the end of his first term. Clock time is not time remembered, and in *The Pyramid* the two often intertwine, run parallel to each other, and even intersect.

What is important is not chronology but that, in two instances, Oliver fails to discover another person. At the close of the first episode, Oliver calls Evie an "undiscovered person"; everyone he encounters remains undiscovered because he makes no attempt to learn their identity. If love, as Iris Murdoch defines it, is the discovery of others, Oliver has discovered no one.

The third episode brings the action to 1963; about thirty years have elapsed since Evie aroused Oliver's passions. Although Oliver is now in his late forties, time has not made him any less superficial, as his summary of the intervening years shows: "The war came on us and the peace; and after years of peace I went back with my family to persuade my mother she must not live alone. . . . I enjoyed a very peaceful war, I'm afraid. We had to have gas ready, of course. But we never used it" (176–77).

In both form and theme, the third episode recalls the radio play *Miss Pulkinhorn*, in which voice-over narration is used to explain the action. At the end of *The Pyramid*, Oliver the narrator recalls his music teacher Clara Cecilia Dawlish ("Bounce"); in the process of remembering her, he supplies the first and last pages of his autobiography.

Time in the final episode is elusive; its restless ebb and flow is heard as if through a seashell. Sometimes the waves of reminiscence cast up fragments of a chronology that must be pieced together. Thus one learns that Oliver at the age of three saw Mr. Dawlish, "a failed musician," smash a phonograph record on a street corner. Bounce has inherited her father's eccentricities, particularly his ambivalence toward music. When Oliver arrives for his first violin lesson at the age of six, he sees a mannish, pipe-smoking woman who arranges his body for the proper positions as if he were a mechanical doll.

As Oliver grows in his love of music, Bounce becomes increasingly apathetic to it. After Henry Williams enters her life, Oliver's music lessons are shortened. He seeks in vain for some recognition from Bounce, some indication that a musical career would be right for him. Instead, Bounce tells him to go into the garage business.

Oliver's music lessons cease when he is eighteen and about to enter Oxford. He sees Bounce again after his first Easter vacation; she had become a pitiful coquette, deliberately driving into ditches to elicit sympathy from Henry. Before returning for his final year at Oxford, he witnesses the penultimate stage of her deterioration when she nonchalantly walks out the front door—nude except for hat, gloves, and shoes.

Oliver's last encounter with her occurs after the war; the chronology is blurred because the reminiscence is reaching its close. She is now a total recluse living in a house overrun with cats. She does not even bother to repeat her usual platitude "Heaven is music," but only discourses on her love for animals, summarizing her view of humanity for Oliver as: "If I could ever save a child or a budgie from a burning house, I'd save the budgie"(179).

Oliver's final recollection of Stilbourne requires explanation because, like so much of the novel, it suggests more than it states. He looks down at the pavement trodden by countless feet, stretches a leg, and begins tapping: "Suddenly I felt that if I might only lend my own sound, my own flesh, my own power of choosing the future, to those invisible feet, I would pay . . . *anything*: but I knew in the same instant that . . . I would never pay more than a reasonable price" (182–83).

There is nothing so characteristic of a small town as the people's movements, particularly the sound of footsteps beating time on the sidewalk and creating a sensible, diurnal rhythm. It seems to echo down a corridor of cement, turning with the bends and curves of the pavement—a practical beat that an indifferent spectator would only find erratic, cacophonous, and finally unaesthetic. For Oliver these footsteps are vestiges of the community. He recalls how Mr. Dawlish "walked, or lunged, rather, through the lanes and streets." When Oliver first met Bounce, he "saw little but Bounce's feet at first." Her "elastic gait" led to her nickname; to Oliver, the walk was inseparable from the person.

When Oliver begins tapping the pavement, he is conjuring up the past. But he realizes that there is a price for remembering and that the price is self-knowledge. He would have preferred a different future for Bounce and himself (perhaps as the successful protégé of a renowned musician) but he would never pay more than "a reasonable price." The price he cannot pay is love; neither he nor Bounce possesses enough. Like the first episode, the third also concludes with a revelation that confirms Bounce's ambivalence toward music and the frustration it caused her. In the garden of her house, which will soon give way to a garage, Oliver finds charred copies of music texts, a shattered Beethoven bust, and a burnt metronome. Like her father, Bounce was also a "failed musician" who in turn failed her pupil.

The Food of Love

Although the three episodes making up *The Pyramid* have a common theme (Oliver's recollections of Stilbourne), a novel should be more than the enclosure of three episodes between two covers, and in one sense, *The Pyramid* is just that. Yet there is a unity informing the three segments, giving them the spine, if not the flesh, of a novel. What unifies them is not exactly love (although the epigraph would lead one to think so) but music which, if approached humanistically, can be an expression of love.

Stilbourne prides itself on being a "musical" community; Oliver's mother played the piano, and his father the violin. The boy was given the usual music lessons, more as an exercise in discipline than in aesthetic appreciation. The young Oliver sought to capture the perfection he encountered through music in human relationships but found instead the traditional disparity between the ideal and the real.

The characters in *The Pyramid* are measured by their response to music. Evie has her own signature—"Boop-a-doop, boop-a-doop." While she enjoys the Chopin that Oliver plays, she can never fully appreciate it. When he tries to explain the technical difficulties of a piece, she can only wantonly pull at his finger. The "music" Oliver would like to make with her is impossible; Chopin and pop are strange bedfellows.

A pretentious community will often attach itself to someone who epitomizes sophistication, dismissing his peculiar behavior as genius. Stilbourne devoted its talent, or lack of it, to the operetta Evelyn de Tracy was directing. In Evelyn, one would have expected some awareness of the humanistic value of music; but his interests are more in transvestism than in art. Bounce became a music teacher because she learned the essentials well enough to teach them; however, she could do nothing for students once they mastered the rudiments. She also had no interest at all in the classics; her musical taste was limited to *Hymns Ancient and Modern.*

Oliver aspired to be a musician but was sidetracked into science by his parents; yet they were a "musical" family. At the end of the first episode, Oliver looked back at Evie after she had slandered him and thought they "might have made something, music perhaps, to take the place of the necessary, the inevitable battle." Music might have its charms but it cannot regenerate the unregenerate. If Bounce had had her way, she would have been a veterinarian; if Oliver had had his, he would have been a musician. Golding, at least, escaped the fate of his characters; he scrambled out from under the net of parental fiat and provincialism.

Chapter Eight
Lost Worlds Revisited
Repetition as the Mother of Studies

Like *The Pyramid, The Scorpion God* (1971) is a collection of three tales, not "short novels" as the dust jacket proclaims. Like its predecessor, *The Scorpion God* contains previously published material, a story "Envoy Extraordinary" (1956). Thus, one-third of *The Scorpion God* is unoriginal as compared to two thirds of *The Pyramid*. The unity of *The Scorpion God* is also thematic rather than structural. The three tales are set in antiquity and depict decadent civilizations; "The Scorpion God" takes place in ancient Egypt, "Clonk Clonk" in a primitive matriarchy, and "Envoy Extraordinary" in Imperial Rome.[1] Finally, like *The Pyramid, The Scorpion God* was a disappointment and left some critics wondering if Golding were not courting the muse of repetition.

In an attempt to recreate an unfamiliar universe and an archaic consciousness, Golding resorts to primitive nomenclature in which a person's name is identical with his or her function or office; he had used a similar technique in *The Inheritors* where the naming process was based on resemblance to natural objects. The king in "The Scorpion God" is Great House; his daughter, Pretty Flower; his jester, the traditional distorting mirror, Liar. Verbal compression, however, can have its drawbacks; calling the reeds that were dipped in paint to color nipples "titsticks" may be acceptable synecdoche in mock rhetoric but in serious fiction it is a stale joke.

Since Golding learned his craft from the Greeks, he begins, as the Greek dramatists did, with a situation approaching the point of no return. In "The Scorpion God," the sun is setting on the Nile, and the gods are enveloped in twilight. During a sacred race, Great House is tripped by Blind Man. The waters rise ominously, threatening to reach The Notch of Utter Calamity that has been carved on the Tree of Life. The prince is bored with mysteries and has no intention of succeeding his moribund father. He yearns to be a female in order to dispense with anthropomorphism and balks at the prospect of an incestuous marriage with his sister. Pretty Flower also has her problems. Like Salome, she must dance for her father, whose waning sexuality is temporarily revived by her gyrations. The day's fiasco, however, has left him impotent; "at least I can still keep the sky up," he mutters (32). As Great House declines, his nemesis, Liar, increases in power, rejecting immortality for hedonism, but he is almost killed when he puts himself up as a candidate for Great House. Head Man dismisses the sacrilege by noting that Liar has a death wish, while Liar escapes and enters Western Civilization as Reason.

Golding has always been ambivalent about the emphasis placed on reason in Western thought. If reason is humankind's distinctive faculty, its preeminence over feelings and emotions is inevitable; yet the enshrinement of reason leads to rationalism, which in turn destroys the myth of the Golden Age. The message of "The Scorpion God" is intentionally opaque: one cannot accept the decadent world of Great House, but the prospect of human reason displacing God is disturbing in a different way. Golding may be trying to say too much. There is no doubt that Greece, where the "river runs round . . . in a ring," will eclipse Egypt; civilizations are bound by the laws of historical inevitability. But Golding's meaning seems to extend beyond the rise and fall of civilizations. He seems to be asking if a decadent anthropomorphism is better than no religion at all, and if the old deities, no matter what they are, are better than humans. One wishes Liar well in his mission, but somehow, like Eliot's aging magus, one would still like to clutch the gods.

In "Clonk Clonk" Golding returns to the divided society of *Lord of the Flies* and presents a matriarchal world so polarized that the sexual roles have been completely reversed. The Sky God yields to the Sky Woman, whom males venerate but whom females reject. Liar-Reason has even made incursions into matriarchies, turning women into rationalists who believe that "the Sky Woman is just the Sky Woman" and "to think anything else is . . . to think like a man" (92); and turning men into homoerotics who seek the warmth of each other's bodies.

This is also a society where initiation into manhood takes the form of ritual rape. When Chimp the cripple returns unexpectedly to the lodge that the women have occupied, they tear off his loincloth and ravish him. At least Chimp avoids the fate of Simon, who also made an ill-timed appearance during a rite. Rape and ritual dismemberment are not the same in Golding. Ravishment is precisely what Chimp needs to restore his manhood. Sex may not save the matriarchy from collapsing, but in the fullness of time the Sky Woman might even grow testicles.

While "Clonk Clonk" has a cynical charm, it is really the tug of war between the fire-watchers and the hunters in *Lord of the Flies* transformed into the battle for sexual supremacy that also results in an armistice when one side gives in. Golding has rewritten his first novel for the Age of Aquarius—the late 1960s when women were female eunuchs and men were prisoners of sex.

From Story to Play—and Back

The third tale, "Envoy Extraordinary," has an interesting history. It was published as a story in 1956 and, two years later, was dramatized as *The Brass Butterfly* (1958).[2] The dramatization will always be better known than the story; it is readily available, easy to stage, and, most important, a far better piece of theatre than literature.

The premise of *The Brass Butterfly* is one that also intrigued the Swiss playwright Friedrich Dürrenmatt: A Roman emperor compounded of myth and history (Golding's emperor is fictitious but suggests something of a cross between Trajan and Marcus Aurelius; the emperor in Dürrenmatt's *Romulus the Great* is Romulus Augustulus, the last of the Caesars) whose scatterbrained exterior conceals a fear of progress and a distrust of humanity. The emperor in *The Brass Butterfly* has retired to Capri where his holiday is interrupted by Phanocles, a Greek rationalist with the detached clarity of vision that his name implies. Phanocles is an inventor and invites the emperor to sample his pressure cooker, steamship, and explosive missile. The emperor is delighted with the pressure cooker but is wary of the others.

The action is further complicated by the rivalry between Postumus, the heir designate, and Mamillius, the emperor's poetic but illegitimate grandson. When the steam engine literally devours Postumus's ships, he uses Phanocles' missile to storm the villa. But Phanocles' sister, Euphrosyne, removes the arming vane, the brass butterfly of the title, causing the projectile to explode and kill Postumus. Mamillius, who has become attracted to Euphrosyne, asks for her in marriage and converts to Christianity. The emperor is left shaken by the day's events and what they presage. For Phanocles, however, a new day is dawning. He envisions a compass, a printing press, and public libraries; he is about to start tampering with the earth's productivity when the wily emperor dubs him envoy extraordinary and sends him on a slow boat to China.

The Brass Butterfly is the sort of playfully serious comedy that a classicist by training and a moralist in outlook would fashion. The techniques of classical drama—the unified action, the Terentian double plot, the messenger's report of off-stage violence—come to Golding effortlessly; they are natural to him and to the play.

Also natural to Golding is polarized vision: the scientist is as single-minded about improving humankind with inventions as the emperor is about saving it with an ineffectual humanism. In this case, however, the polarity does not arise from voices crying out in Dionysian rage or Apollonian despair. Phanocles cannot understand the emperor's conservatism; the emperor, while he cannot accept the consequences of science, knows all too well that it is humans who can transform a steam engine designed for navigation into a dynamo of death. When Phanocles asks what is wrong with man, the emperor gives a one-word reply: "Men."

The emperor's position, at first, baffles and irritates: "There is nothing wrong with man's intelligence. The trouble is his nature." He speaks like a sophist, quibbling about singular and plural because he considers the species a corruption of the genus. He cannot see that a genus requires a species for its realization, and that a species results in divergences. Furthermore, to differentiate between human intelligence and human nature is to ignore the fact that intelligence is part of human nature.

Although the emperor's Platonism is exasperating, the character is sympathetic; he is a saddened humanist, a disbeliever in humanity, a clinger to old gods. In short, the emperor is a Golding self-portrait. Dramatically, the audience accepts the emperor's dilemma because he accepts it himself. If the emperor had merely said that men subvert man, he would just be a wearisome misanthrope. But he goes on to state the familiar thesis that science is amoral and, like everything else, can be used for good or ill.

A thesis play is difficult to resolve, especially a play about the unresolvable. Golding does not give the audience a tidy resolution; however, he does close the wound he has opened by conjuring up the magic of stagecraft to create a twilight that is now more gentle than ominous. A eunuch sings, and harp music filters in from the veranda. The comedy that began with Mamillius diligently working out the metrics of a love poem concludes with the emperor meditating on what scientific discovery will mean for humanity. The day's events have chastened him; he no longer speaks epigrammatically because he is no longer playing high comedy.

Yet the emperor is still a humanist, and the humanist is always cleverer than the literal-minded scientist. While the emperor can laugh at himself and his idealism, he will not be defeated. And so the sweetening of the pill begins. Phanocles will take a slow boat to China, and scientific advancement will be deferred. The audience can breathe more freely, knowing that whenever destruction is imminent, there will always be a deus ex machina, whose forms, as Euripides liked to point out, are many, conceivably including an extended sea voyage for progressives.

The Brass Butterfly has the aura of a dream. Euphrosyne walks about in a trancelike state, claiming she was directed to remove the brass butterfly as if in a dream. In the final scene, the emperor asks Phanocles if he had dreamed the day's events. Seeing (or reading) the play is like being trapped in a dream that threatens to become a nightmare; one is tossed about in waves of fitfulness and then returned to wholeness with the jolt of waking. The emperor has undergone a similar experience; he too is the stuff that dreams are made on. He may have played the fool, but fools, as Erasmus has shown, can be wise. By designating Phanocles envoy extraordinary, the emperor is no longer the proverbial bell without a clapper. The sound is quite resonant.

Chapter Nine
Comprehending Darkness
Let There Be Light

When *Darkness Visible* (1979) was published, it was advertised as the first "new Golding" in more than a decade—a claim that was true if one considers only his novels. Indeed, if one recalls that two of the three episodes comprising *The Pyramid* had been published earlier, *Darkness Visible* was Golding's first bona fide novel since *The Spire.* The new Golding also revealed that he could be as adept at graphic sex and obscenity as any bestselling author. But the new is often a mirror of the old; and if *Darkness Visible* seems unrelated to what preceded it, it is because its contemporary setting, language, and violence have obscured its relationship to the other works. Furthermore, familiar motifs and themes have been reworked, singly and in combination, with such skill that they seem to be appearing for the first time. The truth of the matter is that *Darkness Visible,* published a quarter of a century after *Lord of the Flies,* is really the latter turned inside out, just as *Lord of the Flies* was *The Coral Island* inverted, a *Bacchae* with children.

In the intervening years, Golding moved from fable and myth into the deeper waters of allegory, the form in which he would be most comfortable dealing with the twentieth century. Like most allegories, *Darkness Visible* is multileveled. It is, among other things, Golding's coming to grips with the postwar world; it is also his answer to the critics who have charged him with never having created a memorable female character. To them, he offers Sophy, perhaps the most amoral heroine in contemporary literature. To those who have accused him of hibernating in the past, he replies with a novel that, although it begins in 1940, is set mainly in the 1960s and 1970s. Finally, to those who feel that while he creates literature, he does not write novels that connect with other novels, Golding presents evidence that his reading is no longer limited to the Greeks. *Darkness Visible,* whose title derives from Milton, abounds in allusions to Dante, the Bible, Thomas Mann's *Death in Venice,* and Dostoevsky's *Crime and Punishment.* Anyone doing a critical study of the double in literature will have to include *Darkness*

Visible. The topic that has become a crusade to such writers as Iris Murdoch, Tom Stoppard, and John Barth—language—is equally vital to Golding; for him, the word derives from The Word, and when belief in the *logos,* the Word conceived as God's divine plan, wanes, so does language until it becomes synonymous with feeling. "I think, therefore I am" becomes, as it did in the 1960s, "I am, therefore I feel."

Story/Plot/Myth

Anyone who has written about *Darkness Visible* begins with a synopsis of the plot, even though plot summaries can be an escape from the serious business of criticism. Yet there is no other way to proceed, especially with a novel in which everyone is halved because everyone is someone else's double. The chief danger in summarizing an allegorical novel is that it exposes the narrative shortcomings that stem from a subordination of plot to meaning; in the case of *Darkness Visible,* a summary makes the plot seem disjointed as well as implausible.

The central character of part 1 is a child of unknown parentage discovered walking naked down an East London street during the Blitz. The bombardment has disfigured him; the left side of his face is so badly burned that he looks two-toned. Nameless, the boy is called Matthew Septimus, Matthew the Seventh; his surname, which is variously misspelled, is Windrove. Like the bildungsroman hero, Matty begins his journey into the world where he becomes both the recipient and the cause of evil. His sole consolation is the Bible, portions of which he commits to memory. After a sojourn in Australia, he returns to the mythical Greenfield in England where he had briefly attended school until his implication in a fellow student's death caused him to be expelled.

Matty's book, which covers the period from 1940 to 1967, ends just as he observes the Stanhope twins, Sophy and Toni, in a Greenfield bookstore. Sophy, the eponymous character of part 2, is Matty's converse. Highly intelligent but without any intellectual discipline, a buyer of books who shows no evidence of ever having read them, Sophy pursues a meaningless existence that reflects her belief in a meaningless universe. Ultimately, she evolves into a nihilist and then, with the aid of her hoodlum lover, into a terrorist. The plot that she hatches to kidnap the son of an oil sheik from the school where Matty works as a handyman backfires. Matty is burned to death in the process—his fate impinging on hers, and hers on his, since, as the title of the third part states, "one is one."

The above summary reveals the novel's grid, not its structure; its plot, not its *mythos*. This is the kind of plot that elicits cries of disbelief from those who fail to realize that the plot is merely a point of departure for a troubled meditation on what was once the post-Versailles, then the post-Hiroshima, and now the post-Vietnam world. It is also a world that Golding seems in this novel to have confronted for the first time; a world in which an undeclared war in southeast Asia polarized a nation; a world in which mores suddenly changed and what was private, including pudenda, became public; a world in which violence had become so commonplace that it no longer seemed extraordinary.

If *Darkness Visible* is judged solely on a narrative basis, it would be like subjecting *Twelfth Night* or *The Tempest* to the standards of literary realism. Although Golding's novels abound in realistic detail, they are not realistic novels; one does not "believe" in a Golding novel the way one believes in, say, *Madame Bovary*. After reading a few pages of *Lord of the Flies*, the reader senses that the boys are not really on an island, yet the reader of *Madame Bovary* never doubts that Flaubert's Normandy is a real place. The reason is that Golding approaches plot poetically, beginning with an idea, an image, or a myth; it is an idea that resembles Pope's "naked nature": something to be embellished or dressed up. Golding's embellishments take the form of symbols so archetypal that they result in a polysemous structure where events, even names, admit of myriad meanings. Multiplicity of meaning, however, often conceals a weak narrative foundation, which is certainly the case in *Darkness Visible* where verisimilitude is eroded by coincidence. While authors have traditionally manipulated narrative so that characters can converge at the same place at the same time (e.g., the characters in *Crime and Punishment* being in St. Petersburg within walking distance of each other), the coincidences were conventions—acceptable elements of plot. But what keeps Dostoevsky's and Dickens's coincidences from becoming contrivances is the richness of characterization in which true verisimilitude lies.

In *Darkness Visible,* there is little characterization except for Pedigree the schoolmaster and Goodchild the bookseller, who are authentic types and therefore accessible characters. Matty and Sophy, on the other hand, are conceived so symbolically that, despite Golding's attempts at physical detail, they resist description. What makes the novel a work of art, however flawed, is Golding's ability to impart a symbolic dimension to each aspect of the plot; when the narrative links are weak, the symbolism keeps the concatenation intact. Since *Darkness Visible* is allegory, what are coincidences on the narrative level become interwoven destinies on the allegorical.

Golding expects the reader to take the novel as fiction and auctorial reflection, not singly but conjointly, so that the denotative level (the Blitz, a burned child, twin sisters) exists simultaneously with the connotative (a hell, a burning babe, split personality). Admittedly, this is a tall order, compounded by the inability of the two central characters to evoke empathy. For Sophy one feels revulsion; for Matty, pity. Matty is half human, half spirit; one responds to his human side, to his suffering and persecution, but not to his mysticism, which seems more bedeviled than divinely inspired. The duality inherent in both characters extends to the novel, forcing the reader to discover in its multilayered world that when one layer has been excavated, another appears; and when that has been uncovered, a third emerges. The layers are always different because the archetypes supporting them are self-perpetuating, appearing differently each time.

Dark Pictures

Coleridge wrote that an allegory is "but a translation of abstract notions in picture-language." The allegory of *Darkness Visible* begins with the title taken from Milton's *Paradise Lost;* it comes from his description of hell (1.63) where, despite its fires, darkness alone is visible. The idea is more than paradox; it is oxymoron, the yoking of opposites. Milton's description, inspired by the *Book of Job* where the dead dwell in a place where light is darkness, is profoundly evocative; it suggests an inverted world where fire is dark and burns without light. This, then, is hell: an unnatural state, a place of fiery darkness. *Darkness Visible* is about hell—the hell above the earth, not below it; a living hell in which darkness is visible. Making the earthly hell a mirror image of the Miltonic hell suits Golding's purpose since the characters are all reverse images of each other. The idea of a "living hell," however, is not unique with Golding. Dante would have also concurred that hell is visible, that it can be seen without journeying through its nine circles. Thus Dante plays tricks with time at the end of the *Infer-*

no, reducing the descent into hell to a twenty-four hour period, so that a day in Hell is merely a metaphor for a day on earth.

Since Golding begins the novel with the hell wreaked on London by the Luftwaffe, which leaves a trail of smoke and glare (i.e., darkness visible), the setting is clearly an "infernal city"; even Golding calls it that. The epigraph from Virgil's *Aeneid* (6.266) corroborates it. In English translation, the epigraph reads: "Let me speak what I have heard." These words are the ritual invocation preceding the journey of Aeneas and the Sibyl to the underworld. The Virgilian juxtaposition of hearing and speaking, while quite different in the context of the *Aeneid,* take on a special significance in Golding's novel, which is also about hearing and speaking: hearing voices whose meaning cannot be articulated (Matty) and speaking words whose meanings cannot be communicated (Sophy). *Darkness Visible* is about a modern hell, the hell of incommunicability. It is a hell in which there are those who cannot express what they have heard as well as those who can, but are so mired in the slime of the self that they sink into incoherence.

The Babe from the Bush

The first image in the novel is of a burning bush, a cloud of fiery smoke caused by the bombs. Although the time is 1940, the associations transcend time. First one thinks of the Book of Exodus; but this burning bush is unlike the one through which the Lord spoke to Moses (Exod.3:2): it is lit from within like the mushroom cloud created by the atomic bomb dropped on Hiroshima on 6 August 1945 when the darkness was visible. At Hiroshima, the heart of the bush was fire lighting the darkness. If the twin parallels, ancient and modern, are to meet, it is through the archetypal symbol of fire as a sign from heaven and an instrument of purgation—a symbol that extends from antiquity to the present, acquiring new associations in each period but never losing its primary significance.

Out of the burning bush comes the burning babe. Although a victim of the Blitz, the child with the partially burned face looks more like a victim of Hiroshima. Since the child is first seen walking naked down a street, he recalls another naked child on another street, immortalized in the most famous photograph of the Vietnam war: of the naked child fleeing down a road after the 1972 napalm attack on Trang

Bang village. The child, Matty, is Everychild scarred by war; he is war's burnt offering and a lesson for the survivors.

Matty is partially burned—on the left side; since his face is bicolored, his darkness—the darkness of his heart (to use Golding's phrase from *Lord of the Flies*)—will be partly visible. Although Matty is an innocent victim of war, he is not innocent himself. "There is no innocent work," as Jocelin learned; and there are no innocent people. If they are not scarred by violence, they are scarred by original sin. Thus, in the course of the novel, Matty is responsible for the death of a student, the expulsion of two teachers, and a bookseller's emigration to Canada because of the notoriety resulting from his association with Matty. Yet Matty is the burning babe of Robert Southwell's poem, the Christ born to die for "men's defiled souls." But since Matty is halved, he is only half Christ; the other half is Dionysus. Like Jocelin's cathedral with its pagan foundation and Christian structure, Matty is an amalgam of two traditions. This time, however, the foundation can be seen because the darkness is visible. Since the left side of Matty's face has been burned away, the right side looks darker. In terms of the theory of the bicameral or double brain that seems to have influenced Golding's choice of a bicolored face, Matty's left cerebral hemisphere, which controls his speech, has been severely affected; hence his inarticulateness. On the other hand, his right hemisphere, the one through which bicameral man heard divine voices and exhortations, is intact. Unable to lead, he follows the commands of his voices. Matty is much like Nietzsche's Dionysus—a formless mass that can be lethal or beneficial depending upon what powers act on it. Since there is no possibility of Matty's forming relationships with people, he withdraws into himself and his voices, becomes the victim as well as the herald of apocalypse.

"What's In a Name?"

Like the classical allegorists, Golding uses name symbolism in the Thomistic sense that the name is the consequence of the thing. In Golding, a name's etymology (Jocelin = fool), sound (Lok = look), or association (Piggy, Mountjoy) frequently open up other levels of meaning. The possibilities of "Matthew," while not infinite, are manifold. In view of the major role the Bible plays in the novel, "Matthew" should have some connection with the evangelist particularly since, in writing his diary in the style of a visionary, Matty seems to be composing a kind of gospel. Iconographically, while Mark is portrayed as a lion, Luke as a sacrificial calf, and John as an eagle, Matthew is represented as having the face of a man because he emphasized Christ's humanity.

The connection is fitting. Matty shows a human face, but one that is incomplete; still, it is recognizable, the way extremes are recognizable. Matty is humankind in disunion, spirit severed from matter—each acting independently of the other. On another level, he is paganism and Christianity in disequilibrium. As the unintegrated self, he is our converse but also our kin. He is our mate—"Matey," as an Australian calls him, using the familiar English pub greeting. He is also mateless yet drawn to women, like the Beast to Beauty.[1]

The associations do not stop here. He is also Matthew Septimus, Matthew the seventh—literally, since there were six other children without names. Matthew Septimus takes great delight in the number seven, the mystical number of the Book of Revelation (seven churches of Asia, seven angels, seven gold lampstands, seven seals, seven trumpets, etc.). On another level, Matthew Septimus (Seven) is Matthew: 7, which concludes with Christ's warning against false prophets (Matt. 7:15–23), a category to which Matty belongs. He preaches the gospel of the inarticulate, the inexpressible. What he offers—feeling—is basically good, but it is feeling divorced from words, emotion cut off from reason. He is Matthew Septimus Windrove, a roving spirit, an afflatus, but not a spiritual leader (although he is mistaken for one because of his appearance—a black hat pulled down the side of his face and a black coat that evoke the Phantom of the Opera). Matty cannot even speak the one word that would be his blessing on humanity; it is a beautiful word, which he sings as a single, ethereal note reminiscent of the single note of the sirens in Er's vision of the universe at the end of the *Republic*. The word begins with a consonant followed by a prolonged vowel and ending in a semivowel; the word is "joy," the joy of being, the Dionysian message. Matty's Dionysian gospel is literally "good news" to Apollonians like the schoolmaster Edwin Bell, whose life lacks that joy and who, like Cadmus and Teiresias in the *Bacchae*, rushes to one who promises it. The Dionysian joy that Matty proclaims is basically amoral because Dionysus transcends morality. The Dionysian does not obey the laws of right and wrong because it makes no distinction between them. Thus, to venerate that force, as Aschenbach does in *Death in Venice* or as Dysart the psychiatrist does in Peter Shaffer's *Equus*, is to venerate the lowest form of consciousness. Worse is to succumb to the Dionysian doctrine that feeling is all and that words are useless; yet this is exactly what Bell does, arguing that Shakespeare never published his plays because he distrusted the word—a theory that suggests Bell should return to graduate school.

The Word Unheard

Matty's inability to use language is due partly to his disfigurement, which plastic surgery has failed to correct, forcing him to speak through one side of his mouth; partly to an incomplete education that, together with his asceticism, has discouraged wide reading. Although Matty limits his reading to the Bible, he also limits the Bible to select parts that he transcribes. He favors St. John—the John of Revelation, not the John of the Fourth Gospel, which apparently has had no effect on him. Yet the opening of John's Gospel, "In the beginning was the word," is central to an understanding of *Darkness Visible.* "The word" is *ho logos,* which has many meanings in Greek. John is using "word" in the double sense of "reason" and "speech." The word existing from all eternity is God's plan for the universe, His *logos;* included in that Plan is the incarnation and the One who would become incarnate— Jesus Christ, the Son, the word that became flesh. The Plan must be made known through speech and language; it must be preached and it must be written down. Matty is hardly a suitable evangelist of the *logos* since he can do neither. Although he can write, what he sets down are run-on thoughts in run-on sentences. If the Dionysian ever tried to record its thoughts, the result would be something like Matty's journal.

The Dionysian is also pure will, unrestrained by morality and un- fettered by thought. Since it is unchecked, it is dangerous; in his own way, Matty is as much a menace as Sophy. While a student at Found- lings, he is responsible for the firing of the schoolmaster, Mr. Pedigree, another of Golding's wonderfully ironic names, suggesting tradition but in a double sense. As a former classicist (who has seen better days), he belongs to an illustrious academic family; as a pederast, he belongs to the tradition of the homosexual schoolteacher, a common literary figure (e.g., Lillian Hellman's *Children's Hour,* Robert Anderson's *Tea and Sympathy,* Simon Gray's *Butley*). Although Golding treats Pedigree as a type, right down to the effeminate rhythms of his speech, the schoolmaster evolves into a genuinely moving figure.

Reprimanded for tutoring some of his pupils privately, Pedigree tries to allay suspicion by rebuffing Henderson, his favorite pupil, who was always given access to his room, and according that privilege to Matty, whose ugliness precludes the possibility of gossip. By mistaking Pedigree's invitation for genuine concern, Matty causes Henderson's death, which occurs in the novel's most obliquely narrated incident. Since Matty, whose speech is seldom understood, is the sole witness, he cannot recount what has happened. Thus Golding must step in as omniscient narrator, but even his explanation is unsatisfactory: "Henderson had begged to be let in and been denied and gone reeling on the leads to slip and fall."[2] Matty alludes to Henderson's death in his diary when, returning to Foundlings in 1967, he looks up at the window of Pedigree's old room "where I saw S Henderson come away after I had followed him and waited" (98). Since Matty's gymshoe was discovered with Henderson's body, and since Henderson fell from the roof while trying to get into Pedigree's room, both Matty and Pedigree are dismissed from Foundlings. Clearly, Pedigree was a victim of circumstance.

When Matty is questioned about the gymshoe, he speaks two words, one of which seems to be "Eden" (but is not) and the other, "evil." What Matty said was 'Edom," not "Eden," yet the idea was the same: an actual fall resulting from a symbolic fall—the Fall of Man. The incident, which even confused some of the critics, represents a risk authors run when they chose an inarticulate protagonist, particularly one who is the only witness to a death. Golding gets himself into an even tighter spot by making the key to Henderson's fall a biblical reference that the headmaster explains for the reader's benefit. In a moment of illumination, the headmaster concludes that Matty said "Edom" (as in "Over Edom have I cast out my shoe," Pss. 60:8 and 108:9).[3] Matty, who takes everything literally, cursed Henderson, whom he knew should not be bothering Pedigree, by hurling his shoe at him, causing the boy to lose his balance and fall to his death. Curiously, Matty felt no remorse; in his disobedience, Henderson was evil. It is only Pedigree's disgrace that affects him. When he recalls Pedigree's words, "It's all your fault," he brings his hand down on a spike, leaving a mark that recalls the stigmata.

Mythically, Matty is continuously shifting between Christ and Dionysus, assuming other roles in between—even that of the jealous Zephyr who caused the death of Hyacinthus, his rival for Apollo's love, by blowing the discus that Apollo had thrown so that it would strike the boy. Golding's characters, like Joyce's, transform old myths into new ones. Matty then emigrates to Australia where the significance of the stigma on his hand is reinforced by a mock crucifixion. Attempting to communicate to someone he thinks is an aborigine that he is both thirsty and a Christian, Matty lies down on the ground in a crucifixion pose in imitation of Christ who said, as Pedigree once reminded him, "I thirst." Matty does not receive a wine-soaked sponge on a reed, but instead a foot stamping on his hands plus an almost emasculating kick in the groin. A good Samaritan in the form of a veterinarian comes to his aid—the perfect reductio ad absurdum of Matty's passion and "crucifarce."

Although Matty pays for his literalism, he does not learn from it. One pities him, yet fears him as one fears any blind force. Lacking exegetical ability, he takes biblical passages out of context and applies them literally. If the letter of the law kills, so does the letter of the text. Matty attracts Australian children by building a tower out of matchboxes which he then ignites, causing a fire that leaves some of the spectators burned. While Matty thinks he is building a tower to heaven, he is really erecting a Tower of Babel. Golding knows Matty's capacity for destruction; to discourage empathy, he tosses in sardonic witticisms (e.g., "One of Matty's characteristics was a capacity for absolute inattention") or makes Matty the butt of black humor ("They all look the same to me" is his answer when asked about the "aborigine" who attacked him). When an immigration official attempts to discover if Matty has extrasensory perception, he replies with difficulty: "I feel." It is a moment both moving and terrifying; moving in its candor, terrifying in its implications. It is precisely Matty's feelings that cause such chaos, rising from the Dionysian wellsprings of his being and flowing in an unchanneled flood.

Before leaving Australia, Matty purifies himself in an elaborate ceremony; brandishing a lamp and wearing only a chain of wheels around his waist, he walks into a marsh. It is a syncretic ritual that combines motifs from classical mythology, Christianity, and Buddhism. Although the wheels have been interpreted as penitential millstones, the context requires that they be regarded as tokens of pain and rebirth; or, in combination, as the painful wheel of rebirth in Buddhism. For someone like Matty, who has a medieval conception of the world, the wheel is an instrument of punishment: the infernal wheel (which may go back to Ixion's wheel in the classical afterlife) on which sinners were racked and impaled in medieval descriptions of hell;[4] the wheel on which Catherine of Alexandria was supposedly tortured. Yet the wheel of torture leads to the vision of the eternal wheels: the triune circle of the Godhead with which *The Divine Comedy* culminates.

Although the lamp recalls the golden bough, the symbol of life after death that Aeneas must pluck before he can descend to the underworld, Matty uses it the way a priest might use a monstrance—for benediction. The entire ritual is a parody of the epic descent to the underworld that the hero undertakes so he can return, renewed, to pursue his mission on earth. The hero generally learns something from his descent to the abode of the dead: Odysseus learns what is in store for him when he returns to Ithaca and how he will die; Aeneas is given a glimpse of the future greatness of Rome. Matty's descent is ritual devoid of meaning—for him, at least. But, since Matty's descent is more medieval than classical, it is fitting that it is a descent into slime. The marsh evokes the foul-smelling rivers and swamps that figure so prominently in medieval visions of hell. If Matty's descent is a sloughing off of the past and a bracing for the present, then immersion in slime is peculiarly apt, although Matty does not know it. Contact with slime, with the "muddy centre" is the ideal preparation for returning to the Britain of the mid 1960s—a Britain of anomie and aimlessness, the Britain of Sophy Stanhope.

Dark Wisdom

Just as the point of view shifted in *The Inheritors* when Lok began his preparations for death, so does it shift in *Darkness Visible* when Matty begins his rite de passage. Just as Lok became a "creature," Matty becomes a "he," a "man" as he shakes off Australia's dust and prepares to assume the role of prophet before playing his final part— the burnt offering. This shift enables Golding to move gradually from Matty to Sophy, from victim to perpetrator. For Matty's story to flow into Sophy's, Golding resorts to an ancient technique, one more common in classical comedy than in contemporary fiction: the adjacent houses. In Greek New Comedy and its successor, Roman comedy, the setting was usually a city street fronted by two or three houses. On High Street in Greenfield, to which Matty now returns, Goodchild's bookstore is flanked on either side by Frankley's, the ironmonger's where Matty once worked, and on the other by Sprawson's where Stanhope has a flat and where his twin daughters, Sophy and Toni, live in a converted stable. Later one discovers that Edwin and Edwina Bell, another set of doubles, lives at Sprawson's. At the end of High Street is a park frequented by Pedigree in his pursuit of the young. As the ultimate in dramatic economy, Sophy's room is the scene of a spiritual session conducted by Matty and attended by Bell and Goodchild.

Although Matty knows Sophy only by sight, as do Bell and Goodchild, all their fates become interwoven. "Since they [the Stanhope twins] are everything to each other, they do not need men," Matty writes in his journal as his book ends. But Golding needs them—and Matty—to effect the transition from part 1 ("Matty") to part 2 ("Sophy").

Sophy is the reverse of Matty. While he knows only the Bible (or rather, select parts of it), she is always frequenting Goodchild's bookstore; yet we never know what she reads. While Matty is Dionysian, Sophy is Apollonian—thinking and planning; yet what she thinks and plans has no relation to anything but herself. While Matty is feeling without reason, Sophy is reason without feeling. She is the dark twin; since her name suggests the Greek word for wisdom (*sophia*), hers is a dark wisdom, the wisdom of the ego reflecting on itself and deciding that nothing matters but the self. By making both characters extreme forms of what they symbolize, Golding is again arguing that an immoderate Apollonianism is just as dangerous as an untempered Dionysianism.

In view of the privileges she has received, Sophy's embracing nihilism is a perversion of reason. At the end of the novel, Goodchild, in a voice that is clearly Golding's, inveighs against the young who have turned their back on the treasure that was "poured out" for them. In some ways Sophy is an unredeemed Raskolnikov. Sophy believes that since the world is running down, nothing matters. Early in *Crime and Punishment,* Raskolnikov argues that if everything is permitted, nothing is forbidden; and if nothing is forbidden, nothing is wrong. Although Raskolnikov discovers the folly of absolute freedom, Sophy does not; to her there is no difference between chance and fate, enjoying sex and inflicting violence during it, killing a chick or kidnapping a child.

While Matty is face, Sophy is mouth; one should picture the "inner" Sophy as a giant mouth within the tunnel of the self; she is a female Pincher Martin, who also metamorphosed into pure mouth. Until Sophy appeared, Martin was Golding's vilest character. Through satanic logic, she reduces free will, humanity's greatest gift, to determinism. Her notion of freedom is blind cooperation with nature so that, when a given set of circumstances arises, a mode of behavior results that is so natural, so ineluctible, that one's response is "of course." Sophy came to that conclusion when she killed a dabchick in a stream. While an adolescent might yield to the temptation to throw a stone at a chick straggling behind the brood, he or she would never rationalize the act as nature's cooperating with the human will to wreak destruction. To Sophy, the sight of the chick and the stone on the ground are not separate entities united by chance, but inextricably associated ones united by necessity. What would ordinarily be chance (her being at the stream and the stone's being on the ground when the chick swam by) becomes fate. Yet, paradoxically, she has chosen: "You could choose to belong to people . . . by being good, by doing what they said was right. Or you could choose what was real and what you knew was real—your own self sitting inside with its own wishes and rules at the mouth of the tunnel" (123). In choosing to yield to the dark urges within her and listen to the mouth inside her, she chooses blind determinism, which rules out any possibility of morality. Thus, for Sophy, the reason for not stealing has nothing to do with its being wrong but with its being boring; similarly, the reason for killing a chick is that the means for doing so were readily available.

The most frightening aspect of Sophy's philosophy is its reasoned nihilism. Once free will ceases, the fortuitous becomes the necessary since all is chance. It is purely a matter of numerical accident that 7 July 1977 can be expressed 7/7/77. Because Sophy confuses the contingent with the necessary, she believes that the combination of sevens is deliberate; yet despite her intelligence, she cannot explain why: "I'm not used to putting that kind of knowing into words" (166). Sophy suffers from what the Roman Stoics called *ignava ratio,* "lazy thinking."

On the other hand, when Matty realizes that 6 June 1966 is 6/6/66, 666 symbolizing the Antichrist in the Book of Revelation, he does not rationalize it away as a necessary number. If Sophy were a literal believer in the Book of Revelation, she would have made 6 June 1966 into an apocalyptic date; Matty is surprised that nothing of consequence happens except a birth and a death.

In some ways, *Darkness Visible* is Golding's answer to Anthony Burgess's *Clockwork Orange,* which argues that even the free will of a rapist thug must be respected and that any attempt to diminish his freedom of choice through conditioning is a violation of human rights. Golding's Sophy is an even more frightening phenomenon than Burgess's Alex. Sophy chooses to be "weird," and in so doing, chooses the unnatural. Everything follows with a perverse logic from that choice: Sophy will bring darkness into a world where there should be light. To return for a moment to St. John's Gospel, she will be the darkness that does not comprehend the light (John 1:5). Sophy has made a free choice, a decision—but not a human decision; while it may be a choice, it is not an act of free will since an act of free will is a human act; there is nothing human about willing weirdness.

In terms of Dantean morality, the morality Golding is following, Sophy is guilty of malice, a sin so great that it is punishable in the eighth and ninth circles of hell. Malice is willing evil to another, thus perverting a faculty (reason) that makes humankind unique. By turning terrorist, Toni, the "fair" twin, commits an even graver sin of malice: treachery against her country, which is punishable in the ninth circle. Each twin is an extension of the other; each is the other's double. They are two-toned (Golding's pun on "Toni") just as Matty's face is two-toned. Matty, however, causes evil accidentally since he cannot will it. Toni and Sophy choose what they do; hence, in combination, they represent ultimate evil, willed evil.

Although the twins pursue separate paths, they are reunited in the kidnapping attempt. Ostensibly, the motive is ransom money, but that was no more Sophy's real reason than Raskolnikov's was financial gain in killing the pawnbroker. In a sense, their motives are similar: to dare the impossible, to perform what André Gide called the gratuitous act that raises the self above the ordinary level. Dostoevsky, however, does not attribute Raskolnikov's problems to his upbringing; Golding does, not directly, but by placing such an emphasis on Sophy's family life that she seems a product of it. By relegating her to the category of unloved child, Golding implies that she turned to nihilism and violence because she was denied parental affection. After Sophy's mother ran off to New Zealand with a lover, her father took a succession of mistresses, known to his daughters as "aunties," and brought them to his flat while Sophy and Toni retreated to a converted stable. In an episode as erotic as it is perverse, Sophy tries to seduce her father; her breasts rise beneath her blouse "in a sign as clear as if it had been shouted" (186). Coyly, she asks what he does for sex, now that he no longer has a mistress. "I masturbate," he hisses. Stung, she replies: "Don't we all?"

This is the only time that Sophy seems real; for a moment one pities her. But far too often she is like one of Dante's damned, a type of sin rather than a character. This is because *Darkness Visible* has the outward form of a novel but is really a meditation couched in fiction; a meditation on moral relativism and the seeming collapse of standards that occurred in the mid and late 1960s when values like patriotism, the preeminence of the liberal arts, marriage and the family were questioned and in some cases replaced by alternatives.

Golding was not the only novelist to be troubled by the sudden switch from Apollonian to Dionysian. In his novel *The Sunlight Dialogues,* John Gardner portrays the suddenness with which the Apollonian can devolve into the Dionysian through the central character, Taggert Hodge, a once successful lawyer whose wife's madness drives him to the edge where the counterculture facilitates the plunge. In 1966, Hodge returns to his hometown, looking like a Jesus freak and speaking the polyglot of the 1960s; an overage flower child, he is arrested for painting "love" near the entrance to the New York State Thruway. Both *The Sunlight Dialogues* and *Darkness Visible* characterize the 1960s as a Dionysian age, not in the sense that it epitomized tragic wisdom (which is the Dionysian at its highest) but tragic waste. The disregard for universals led to a devaluation, and then a transvaluation, of values until for every Apollonian value there arose a Dionysian antivalue. Both Gardner and Golding portray a period in which good and evil were no longer two sides of the same coin but two superimposed faces on a coin that always came up heads. Hodge, the sunlight man, is as Janus-faced as the sixties, or as the original Dionysus, who looked forward to Greece and backward to Asia. Hodge parodies the New Testament ("Father, forgive them! They know not whom they screw!") just as Matty parodies the Book of Revelation, and Sophy existentialism. What Gardner embodies in one character, Golding splits into two.

Taggert Hodge is at least fleshed out; Matty and Sophy are not. In their own way, Matty and Sophy have exceeded the human norm— Matty by circumstance, Sophy by choice. Since they are extreme forms of what they represent (divine madness and diabolical self-fulfillment), they remain largely unknowable except for rare moments when the human surfaces in them. Sophy is a special problem; one has the feeling that Golding lavished so much attention on the external aspects of her character because he could not fathom her interior. Golding knew little of swinging London or international terrorism; consequently, he presents a conventional picture of each. If the title story of Nadine Gordimer's *Something Out There* is representative, terrorists do not explain themselves or their philosophy; they act rather than talk. And if they

did talk, they would express themselves far less rhetorically than Sophy, who believes simplicity is achieved by the outrageous.

There are times when Sophy seems to be Golding's whipping post.
Sophy personifies the 1960s, which to Golding was a dark age. What
especially bothered him about the period was that the return to simplicity that the Aquarians advocated was really a reversion to primitiv-
ism whose chief exponents were the guru and the radical. With the
guru came the flower children, Woodstock nation, and the pacifists;
with the radical came the student militants, the Weather Under-
ground, Students for a Democratic Society, and the Red Brigades. In
the novel the guru is Matty; the radical, Sophy. The difference between
them is that Matty may be less dangerous than Sophy. Still, if unchecked, each can destroy civilization because each is indifferent to the
word. In contradistinction to Sophy's "I hate," there is Matty's "I feel";
neither philosophy will keep the torch of knowledge lit.

Simon and Sebastian

There is no mean between the extremes of Matty and Sophy, although, for a time, it seems that Sim Goodchild might be. Goodchild
is an adult Simon in postcolonial Britain where Sikhs and Pakistanis
have settled in villages that were once Anglo-Saxon and where mosques
are a reminder of a pluralistic world. While Goodchild finds change
difficult, he has not become a racist or a bigot; he still believes in the
power of the word and the ability of language to express thoughts
clearly, which is more than Edwin Bell does. Bell is so mesmerized by
Matty that he starts questioning the efficacy of the word and the value
of literature; because he believes Matty is a guru belonging to the new
wave of Eastern mystics, he takes up reading *The Bhagavad Gita,* although Matty knows nothing about it.

When Bell proposes a nocturnal meeting with Matty, Goodchild,
although skeptical of religious fads, agrees to attend. For his efforts,
he hears something akin to the music of the spheres—or rather, one
note of it, which is all Matty can manage. Goodchild and Bell pay the
price for their rendezvous, however. Unaware that the meeting place
is under police surveillance, they discover that the session has been
videotaped; it ends up on local television. The notoriety is so great that
Bell is dismissed from his post and Goodchild is forced to emigrate to
Canada.

When Bell proposes to write a history of the affair, Goodchild replies with Henry Ford's aphorism that history is bunk. Again one hears Golding's voice as the author absolving himself for being unable to probe the psyches of radicals or mystics, offering instead a case study. While one never learns what creates a radical (it must be more than lovelessness) or a mystic (clearly more than disfigurement), one at least learns something about the nature of each, especially that they are related as extreme forms of behavior; "One is One" the title of part 3 states. Yet this is a kind of knowledge—the kind at which Golding excels: cosmic knowledge, the knowledge of universals, the knowledge of myths, the knowledge of self.

Curiously, the one character who experiences self-knowledge is the least likely candidate for it: Sebastian Pedigree. Although Golding has put some of his convictions into Goodchild's mouth, that character is as incomplete as Sophy and Matty. Goodchild is out of place in the nuclear age; while his allegiance to books is admirable, it is only to be expected from a bookseller. Goodchild lacks the insight into himself and his age that reading traditionally provides.

Pedigree, on the other hand, knows what he is: a pederast who pursues children "just for affection . . . a touch." Although Bell calls him a "filthy old thing" and the community considers him a menace, Pedigree says (and Golding would agree) that what he has done is "nowhere near the worse" compared to hijackings and bombings done supposedly for the highest of motives. While others in the novel are victims of circumstance, Pedigree is a victim of love—Matty's love that backfired. Yet like Willy Loman in Arthur Miller's *Death of a Salesman*, who learns before his suicide that his son Biff really loves him, Pedigree realizes the same about Matty.

In an ending imitative of *Death in Venice*, Pedigree dies. He is summoned to death not, however, by a handsome boy but by the spirit of Matty in a shimmer of sunlight. It is fitting that Matty should come for Pedigree; they are doubles, so much so that when he was alive, Matty was literally Pedigree's shadow. Each is a grotesque—one a mystical Dionysian, the other an Apollonian gone to seed. In an extremely complex passage, death and transfiguration occur simultaneously. The sunlight enveloping Matty becomes a fire of metamorphosis like that in Yeats's "Sailing to Byzantium" where aged flesh is melted into golden birds. Similarly, Matty's once bicolored face acquires a gilded homogeneity as he is transformed into an object of art, an icon of eternity.

Matty appears to Pedigree in the form of a peacock. Recall that, in

The Spire, Gilbert sculpts a head of Jocelin that gives the priest a bird-like look. By implication, Jocelin is a bird of prey, the inverse of the dove emblematic of the Paraclete. Metamorphosis has given Matty the appearance of a peacock. In Christian iconography, the peacock symbolizes the resurrection because its plumage renews itself annually. The "eyes" that Pedigree sees are the iridescent spots in the peacock's tail that have been variously interpreted as symbolic of eternity and Christ's wounds.[5] They also suggest the *cauda pavonis* ("tail of the peacock"), an important concept in medieval alchemy. The *cauda pavonis* expressed the rainbow colors that appeared near the end of the alchemic process; the fact that Matty is enveloped in an aura of gold, the goal at which alchemy aimed, and that he comes for Pedigree in the form of a golden peacock means that Pedigree too is ready for transformation and the journey to eternity.

Pedigree, however, is reluctant to embark on that journey. When he asks "why?", Matty replies ("but not in human speech") with another one-word answer: "freedom." It is freedom from desire, the kind of freedom Pedigree yearns for; yet when offered it, he resists, clutching the ball he used to entice the young. Freedom means the loss of the ball and all it represents: touching, affection. Pedigree wants release; when it is within his grasp, he clings to the last vestige of life— a ball. This is the one human act in the novel. In fighting transfiguration, he is fighting death; and in so doing, Pedigree gives *Darkness Visible,* brilliant as it is, the one ingredient it had been lacking: humanity.

Chapter Ten

Ship of Letters

A Return to the Fold

Rites of Passage (1980) appeared the year after *Darkness Visible;* like *The Inheritors,* which followed *Lord of the Flies* by a year, *Rites of Passage* is so seamless in its construction that it seems to have been spun rather than written. It therefore comes as no surprise to learn that it was written in a brief but concentrated period of time, perhaps in the four weeks that it took the author to write *The Inheritors.* Unlike *The Inheritors,* which, for all its acclaim, never enjoyed the popularity of *Lord of the Flies, Rites of Passage* was a bestseller, garnering as well the Booker-McConnell prize as the best novel of 1980. It was the early 1960s revisited: Golding became a public figure, interviewed on British television, and accorded the full man-of-letters treatment.

The Inheritors may be Golding's favorite novel, but *Rites of Passage* is his most perfect: it is what readers and critics want of an author: a coda (even if other works follow), a personal as well as a literary summing up. This is a work of such density that, to be appreciated, it must be approached layer by layer, even if its complexity must be disturbed to reveal its art. In some ways, it is familiar; old themes (the novel as personal reply, the Apollonian-Dionysian *agon,* the Greek tragic structure, the denouement as revelation) are restaged but within a new setting in which the familiar has regained its "innocence," as Golding might say.

The Novel as Answered Question

Except for *Darkness Visible,* Golding has willingly discussed the genesis of his novels. Generally, they grew out of his dissatisfaction with received ideas, accepted views, unsatisfactory accounts, or ambiguous sources. *Rites of Passage* originated as an attempt to explain a phenomenon that had long troubled the author: the large number of medically unexplainable deaths in both literature and life. Prime examples include Lucy in Sir Walter Scott's *Bride of Lammermoor,* the inspiration for Donizetti's opera *Lucia di Lammermoor,* in which the heroine goes mad on her wedding night, kills her husband, and dies shortly thereafter; Fiers in Chekhov's *Cherry Orchard* who, at the end of the play, lies down on a sofa and presumably dies; Wagner's great trio—Elsa in *Lohengrin,* Elisabeth in *Tannhäuser,* and Isolde in *Tristan und Isolde*—who expire most unscientifically: Elsa swoons, Elisabeth no sooner finishes singing her prayer to the Virgin than her bier is carried on stage, and Isolde, after completing the "Liebestod," collapses on Tristan's body.

Clarissa Harlow, the heroine of Richardson's *Clarissa,* suffers indignities that would have left another traumatized but not dead. One might say Clarissa died of shame, although that is somewhat of an oversimplification; shame might be an explanation, but not a scientific one. At least Richardson supplied a context for his heroine's shame: her ordeal in the brothel, her rape by Lovelace, and her subsequent mistreatment by her family. But what of the shame-ridden who are not fortunate enough to have a novelist explain their deaths? What about the clergyman whose strange death was recorded in a life of Wellington that Golding happened to read? It seems that, in 1796, after three days at sea, a clergyman began to act in such a debauched manner that, when he realized what he had done, he withdrew to his cabin, refusing food and company. Even Lord Wellington's ministrations were of no avail, and a short time later the clergyman died.

Although Golding never cited *Clarissa* as one of his influences, it clearly is; the clergyman in *Rites of Passage* dies from the same interrelated factors of sexual defilement, sullied honor, and persecution that caused Clarissa's death. Golding, however, reached that conclusion only after he had placed the incident within the context of eighteenth-century life and letters; this enabled him "to invent human circumstances to make us understand how a man could die of shame."

Choosing a Form

Art is never as simple as answering a question; the answer must take on form—first in terms of genre, then in terms of structure. Writing fiction involves a series of choices, one of which is the mode of narration. Golding's source solved the problem of genre and setting; *Rites of Passage* would be a historical novel set on board a ship. He changed the exact dates from 1796 to 1812–13, a change that poses a slight problem, as we will see later. Still, it is clear that he wanted the reader to imagine the action taking place in the early nineteenth century as a new order in society and literature is beginning.

In *The Rhetoric of Fiction,* Wayne Booth argues that no narrative is unmediated; someone is telling the story, whether it is the implied author, a narrator-agent, an "I," or several "I's." If the "I's" are letter-writers whose correspondence constitutes the plot, the result is an epistolary novel, one of the dominant types of eighteenth-century fiction.

Although *Rites of Passage* is set at the dawn of English romanticism, the characters are still in the sunset of neoclassicism. Thus, if Golding wishes to be authentic, as he clearly means to be, he must use an eighteenth-century model; since the action takes place at sea, the model must be a journey novel; since it is an account of a voyage written both as a diary and as a letter, the narrative mode must be epistolary. One of the best examples of an eighteenth-century journey novel that also happens to be an epistolary novel in which the same event is told through letters from different points of view is Smollett's *Humphry Clinker.* Since *Rites of Passage* consists of two complementary versions of the same voyage, it is clear that *Humphry Clinker* was one of Golding's many influences.

There is, however, a major difference between the two works. *Rites of Passage* is based on an actual event; it therefore embodies two traditions, fiction and chronicle. Consequently, Golding is able to preserve the diarist quality of one of his sources, Scawen Blunt's *My Diaries: Being a Personal Narrative of Events, 1888–1914,* which alludes to Wellington's attempt to buoy up the spirits of the person who later died.

Golding has worked out a form evocative of the eighteenth century yet accessible to the modern reader. Basically, the novel is a journal the narrator keeps at the request of his patron; within that journal is a letter that the clergyman who died of shame had written to his sister. While the clergyman's letter may have been inspired by Joseph's letters to his sister Pamela in Fielding's *Joseph Andrews,* the resemblances cease with the inspiration. Joseph's bedside encounter with Lady Booby is a far cry from the clergyman's escapade with a young sailor.

Since the letter and the diary enjoyed the status of literature in the eighteenth century, it was perfectly logical to make the main narrative a journal a traveler is keeping—not for himself but for the godfather-patron through whose generosity he is en route to the Antipodes where an administrative post awaits him. While there is no exact eighteenth-century analogue for a journal novel written for a patron, there are two traditions that Golding has combined to create his narrative form: the

novel dedicated to a patron (Sterne's *Tristram Shandy*) and the practice
of supplying a patron with reports as Samuel Pepys did for his, Edward
Montagu.

Character

Once he found an authentic form, Golding had to invent authentic
characters to inhabit it. This was more difficult since Golding conceived *Rites of Passage* as a dark odyssey, a voyage to the other side of
the world. The controlling metaphor, then, is one of inversion, where
things stand in antipodal relation to each other; where good and evil,
law and lawlessness are reversed. While shipboard conditions in the
novel may suggest Smollett's *Roderick Random,* and while Golding's
Captain Anderson may seem reminiscent of one of Smollett's sea dogs,
we are really a long way from the Jolly Tars. Golding's characters may
appear familiar, but it is their underside that we generally see, as one
would expect from an antipodal point of view. Captain Anderson is a
sea dog turned tyrant; the Reverend Colley is the Vicar of Wakefield
(or Fielding's Parson Adams) as pederast.

The main narrator, Edmund Talbot, has the snobbish airs of Smol-
lett's Jery in *Humphry Clinker,* the sexual proclivities of Richardson's
Lovelace, and Mr. Shandy's philological sense of humor. One of the
passengers, Miss Granham, is a governess—a familiar type in Jane
Austen's novels. In fact, at the end of *Rites of Passage,* marriage to a
freethinker, Mr. Prettiman, saves her from the "governess-trade," as
Jane Austen called it in *Emma* where marriage to Frank Campbell saves
Jane Fairfax from a similar fate. Interestingly, the sole reference to
Emma in *Rites of Passage* proves something of a gaffe. One of the passengers in Golding's novel is Zenobia Brocklebank, who is masquer-
ading as a lithographer's daughter but is really a doxy, just as her
"father" is a whoremonger exporting her to Australia where she will
continue in prostitution. If Zenobia did not have her own form of
patronage, she might have ended up in a brothel similar to the one
where Lovelace raped Clarissa. But Zenobia experiences something
akin to Clarissa's ordeal when Talbot takes her in his cabin, forcing
himself on her not unwilling body.

When Talbot discovers an illiterate letter from an ardent sailor (later
revealed to be Billy Rogers, the anti-Billy Budd), he claims Zenobia
"had an attack of the Emmas,"[1] meaning that she must have flirted
with Billy as Emma did with Mr. Knightley. Yet, if the time of the

novel is 1812–13, Talbot could not have read *Emma* (1816) since it had not yet been published. Regardless, Golding's characters are either inversions or composites of eighteenth-century and Regency types; if the characters of the eighteenth-century novel are inverted, so too are the conventions, one of which is parental or filial recognition. This convention requires the parent's learning the identity of the child, or vice versa, toward the end of the novel (Bramble's learning about Humphry in *Humphry Clinker,* Don Rodrigo's discovering that Roderick is his son in *Roderick Random,* Tom Jones's finding out who his parents are in *Tom Jones*). One of the revelations at the end of *Rites of Passage* is that Captain Anderson's father was a noble. But it is not Anderson who learns this; he has known it since childhood. It is Talbot who does—and from a social inferior at that.

Not only has Golding inverted an eighteenth-century convention; he has also inverted an eighteenth-century plot. When Talbot hears Summers use a letter name, Lord L., for Anderson's father, he remarks that the technique is pure Richardson; he might also have said pure Fanny Burney, for the situation derives from her novel *Evelina,* in which Sir John Belmont abandons his wife when he discovers she has no fortune, with the result that their daughter Evelina is brought up by a clergyman. Evelina at least learned principles from her guardian; Anderson learned only contempt for the clergy. Had fate not intervened, Anderson would have inherited his father's title. Unfortunately, Lord L. needed money; as a result, Captain Anderson's mother, Lord L.'s mistress, was married off to a minister, who acquired a son along with a wife, just as Lord L. acquired a wife along with a fortune.

The Novel as Social Microcosm

It must have occurred to Golding that double narration, in which the two narrators belonged to two different classes, admitted of various possibilities—epistemological, literary, and social. The knowledge Talbot's journal cannot supply, Colley's letter to his sister can; and what neither can express in the text, Golding can express in the subtext. The two documents, then, are like mirrors reflecting the same image, except that neither mirror can render the image exactly as it is; like the correspondents in *Humphry Clinker,* Talbot and Colley mirror class realities as well as action.

Golding's interest in class distinction is a natural outgrowth of his fascination with the Apollonian and the Dionysian; while he tried to combine class and bipolar morality before (e.g., *Lord of the Flies* and *The Spire*), he was never so successful as in *Rites of Passage*. The ship with its demarcated quarterdeck, afterdeck, and lower deck is British society in miniature with its upper, middle, and lower classes—each with its gradations and corresponding types. The tripartite division also recalls Plato's ideal state in *The Republic* which, if sketched, would be a pyramid with artisans at the base, auxiliaries in the middle, and guardians at the apex. *Rites of Passage* answers the question that students commonly ask about Plato's utopia: what would happen if an artisan tried to enter the auxiliaries, if a guardian fell in love with an artisan, or a guardian proved incompetent? The wonderfully Apollonian—or, in Nietzsche's view, optimistic—order would crumble, as indeed it does on board ship in Golding's novel; as indeed it did in Britain with the Industrial Revolution and the rise of a new middle class. It crumbles because it is artificial.

At the outset of the voyage, class distinctions start breaking down because of the disparity between the nature of the passengers and their social rank. On the surface, Captain Anderson behaves like a typical eighteenth-century sea captain, the kind of autocrat that Fielding described in his *Journal of a Voyage to Lisbon*. His separating the quarter-deck from the rest of the ship by a white line of demarcation is more indicative, however, of an aristocrat than of an autocrat. He has made the quarterdeck his estate, a sacred precinct. While Talbot and the others would brand such behavior as arrogant in a sea captain, they overlook it in a noble. Yet from Anderson's point of view, he is a noble; that he is not called Lord, as his father had been, is a caprice of fortune. Anderson acts as if he were son of a lord, not the son of a minister; his behavior, then, is consistent with his father's rank. That he should scorn clergymen, especially someone like Colley who moved up the social ladder while Anderson was forced to move down, is understandable.

Ironically, Anderson, Colley, and Talbot are all products of patronage, but in different ways. Anderson could never have advanced to skipper had it not been for Lord L.; Colley would have remained a country parson had it not been for the Lord Bishop; Talbot would have been an educated philanderer if his godfather had not decided to play Lord Chesterfield. None of them is what he seems; but then, no one is in *Rites of Passage*. On the good ship *Britannia,* people belong anywhere they can find or carve a niche.

The ship is no sooner afloat than class and privilege are ignored.

Colley vomits on Talbot, thereby making them equals. Emigrants from the lower deck attend the service Colley conducts in the saloon, thus committing a social impropriety. Colley, confident that his position allows him run of the ship, visits the quarterdeck, only to be humiliated by Captain Anderson for overstepping his bounds. Yet when Talbot invades the inner sanctum, he is not berated. In Anderson's eyes, Talbot is a gentleman and therefore an exception to the rule. In his search for a cozy spot for love-making, Talbot puts aside his class consciousness, descends into the bowels of the ship, and talks to the scurvy crew; lust knows no boundaries. As it happens, Talbot need not have debased himself by going down into the hull; an unexpected opportunity arises during the crossing of the equator when he is able to signal to Zenobia that he is retiring to his cabin. When she arrives, he "boards" her in a manner too mutual for rape, too aggressive for seduction. Like Lovelace, Talbot is a gentleman ravisher who commits literary fornication as his bookshelf collapses, revealing his picaresque taste—*Gil Blas* and *Moll Flanders*.

Ignorance of one's social and moral nature leads to self-delusion. In his obsession with the gentlemanly ideal, Talbot believes Lieutenants Cumbershum and Deverel are officers and gentlemen; to Talbot, a gentleman is a social, not a moral, designation. But in their baiting of Colley, the officers behave like prefects in a British public school, treating the minister as if he were an underling to be used for their pleasure. Only Lieutenant Summers is what he is: a "good man," as Talbot remarks sarcastically. Yet Summers is good; Talbot, who thinks Summers is a gentleman, is startled to hear the lieutenant admit he is just a common seaman who advanced by his own ability. Summers did not need a godfather, a father, a whoremonger, or a bishop. He had himself; he represents the new order.

The Novel as Literature

Despite his godfather's desire to hear all, Talbot vows to be selective, keeping his journal in the manner of Fielding rather than Richardson but not knowing that he is more like Richardson's Lovelace than the son of Lord Chesterfield. Thus, at the very beginning, Golding acknowledges that he is operating according to the literary principle of selectivity. The goal, however, is the classical combination of the select and the representative; that is, selective representation, a portrait of what is abiding and unchanging in human nature.

Talbot begins by separating selectivity and representation, assuming that the former can be achieved by a judicious analysis of events and the latter by their elegant rendering in chronological order. But as the shipboard drama unfolds, the diurnal approach is abandoned. Days are missed, and days once numbered are designated by Greek letters (alpha, beta), general headings ("the next day"), expressions of puzzlement ("?"), and finally the ampersand ("&").

While Talbot fancies himself a writer (and his prose can be dazzling), he is essentially a storyteller with an unfinished story. He has not solved the mystery of Colley's death; to accomplish his goal and "conceal nothing," he needs Colley's letter. But the letter is also incomplete; it lacks a beginning and an end, because Colley has died before finishing it. Between them, the two narrators can provide an introduction, a rising action, and a climax—but not a denouement.

That one uses terms like "rising action" and "denouement" in discussing *Rites of Passage*—terms more appropriate to drama than to the novel—implies that, lodged within the narrative, is a play. Golding has never denied his thematic debt to Greek tragedy, but it was not until the publication of *Rites of Passage* that he also admitted that the form of his fiction was also conceived under Greek influence: "I think of the shape of a novel, when I do think of a novel as having a shape, as having a shape precisely like a Greek drama. . . . So the Greek tragedy as a form, a classical form, is very much there."[2]

Golding's fifteen-year immersion in Greek literature and his mastery of E. R. Dodds's edition of the *Bacchae* might naturally result in fiction structured as tragedy. Yet, *Rites of Passage* is primarily a novel; Colley's story gives it a tragic rhythm, and Talbot's narrative a fictional form. Reading the novel is like viewing a holograph of Golding's mind: the novelist and the tragedian working at first separately, then together. The tragedy is Colley's; it is Colley who undergoes the tragic pattern of *agon* (the clash with Anderson), *pathos* (degradation), and *sparagmos* (mental deterioration and death).

Golding, however, does not stop there. While all his novels have the rhythm of the tying and loosening of the knot, Golding's loosening tends to be either a deus ex machina or a revelation, often the divulging of an Ibsenian secret (Jocelin's purchased deanship, Evie's incest, Captain Anderson's parentage). Since *Rites of Passage* is an answer to a hitherto unsolved death, the revelation is the denouement, and the novel concludes like a detective story—like *Oedipus Tyrannus*, the first detective story. The mystery of Colley's death is solved: the minister died of

shame because he realized that, in a state of inebriation, he had performed fellatio on Billy Rogers. The circumstances are such, however,
that the revelation must be reported like the messenger's account of
offstage violence in Greek tragedy. The revelation is also a matter of
chance; Talbot would never have known why Colley died if Prettiman
had not told him. By making the gentleman-narrator dependent on an
inferior, Golding is emphasizing Talbot's limited knowledge and his
unreliability as well as his unfamiliarity with the argot he has boasted
of mastering.

Prettiman tells Talbot that he heard Rogers brag about getting a
"chew off a parson." Talbot at first does not make the connection with
fellatio because Summers, who knows the vernacular, put sheaves of
tobacco leaves in Colley's cabin after his death; Summers hopes that if
the phrase were used again, genteel passengers like Miss Granham
might think Colley was addicted to the heathen vice of "chewing"
tobacco. But that is not all Talbot learns from Summers; he also learns
the truth about Anderson's parentage. Thus, the most important pieces
of information gleaned in the novel have come to Talbot from others.
In tragedy, knowledge of others should produce knowledge of self, as
it does in *Oedipus Tyrannus* where knowledge of (and from) others brings
about the protagonist's self-knowledge or *anagnorisis.*

But neither Talbot nor Colley is Oedipus; each learns something
(Talbot why Colley died, Colley what he is), and each experiences *anagnorisis;* but the effect is not as satisfactory as it is in Sophocles' play.
Golding is pushing *anagnorisis* to the limit; since the story is told by
two narrators, a tragic figure and a diarist, perfect *anagnorisis* would
occur only if the diarist learned something substantial from the fate of
the tragic figure. Talbot learns something, but since he is a superficial
observer, his knowledge is superficial. At the end, he can only say with
scribal certitude: "In the not too ample volume of man's knowledge of
Man, let this sentence be inserted. Men can die of shame." It is doubt-
ful that Talbot realizes he was indirectly responsible for Colley's fate.
If Talbot had not tried to embarrass the captain by requesting a religious service for the passengers (a matter to which Talbot was totally
indifferent), Colley's vulnerability would not have been so cruelly ex-
posed, nor would his evangelism have had an opportunity to manifest
itself. Once Colley plays the priest, he is typecast for the role of
scapegoat.

The scapegoat rituals in *Rites of Passage* have their antecedents in the
Dionysian worship as depicted in the *Bacchae* in which Pentheus is first

teased by Dionysus, then encouraged to dress as a Bacchant prior to his dismemberment and death. In the novel, the ritual occurs in two phases: the interrupted "badger bag" and its resumption in the hull where it culminates in a sexual act. As Virginia Tiger notes, the badger bag, a term that even Talbot cannot find in his maritime dictionary, refers to the ceremonial hazing conducted by the sailors in honor of Neptune during the equatorial crossing.[3] Generally, it was a harmless affair with the crew playing tricks on the passengers. Still, activities such as trick or treat and harvest celebrations can have their dark side, as movies (the Halloween sequence in *Meet Me in St. Louis, Halloween*) and popular fiction (Thomas Tryon's *Harvest Home*) have shown. During the crossing, Colley becomes the equatorial fool, brought before a sailor dressed as Neptune who brandishes a trident, thus taking on the appearance of a devil as well as a sea divinity. Smeared with excrement and immersed in stagnant water, Colley the equatorial fool becomes the equatorial scapegoat. It is only a gunshot from the compassionate Summers that brings the grotesquerie to a close. Ironically, Talbot, who has vowed to "conceal nothing," did not even witness the event since he was tumbling Zenobia in his cabin.

Ritual worship has become ritual defilement; it soon becomes ritual orgy. The final stage might never have occurred if Colley, in his eagerness to convert the seamen who had abused him (in effect, turning the other cheek), had not descended into the hull, clad in his ecclesiastical attire. Like Pentheus in the *Bacchae* who dresses as a woman, Colley puts on clerical dress which, to the crew, appears feminine. Pentheus is not the only role Colley is playing; he steps into another part, also Euripidean—Silenus. Colley is too pathetic to continue as Pentheus. His degradation is partly masochistic, partly the effect of misguided evangelism in which his mission to convert the heathen merges with his unconscious desire to partake of their heathen ways. Golding has another play in mind, Euripides' *Cyclops*, which is not a tragedy but a satyr play; in it, the drunken Cyclops carries off and rapes Dionysus's follower Silenus. Plied with rum and stripped of his clerical garb, Colley is ready for anything, including fellatio. Yet, in a tragically ambivalent way, the experience was liberating, for Colley emerges from the fo'c's'le crying "joy, joy," perhaps the first he has ever known.

The Dionysian *eleutheria* is only momentary; it leaves Colley transported and shouting "joy," which was also Matty's message to the world in *Darkness Visible*. Just as the joy that Matty brought was only temporary, so too are the effects of Dionysian intoxication; it may offer liberation from repression, but in Colley's case, it is liberation for one who had previously practiced sublimation and who cannot cope with newfound sexual freedom. Intoxication has brought destructive self-knowledge, the kind more associated with the modern than with the classical stage. Colley's is the self-knowledge that destroys; it is the kind that caused Blanche du Bois's husband in Tennessee Williams's *A Streetcar Named Desire* to kill himself after Blanche made her accusation of homosexuality; it is the kind that, in Arthur Miller's *A View from the Bridge*, led to the death of Eddie Carbone, who was forced to see himself as the would-be lover of his niece. In the classical tradition, ignorance—not knowledge—is destructive because ignorance is a state that is unnatural to rational beings motivated by a desire to know. Colley needed self-ignorance to survive; losing its comforts, he dies, willing his death just as Miller's Carbone willed his, turning Marco's knife upon himself.

There is a further similarity between *A View from the Bridge* and *Rites of Passage*. Miller frames Carbone's death within a classical setting that even requires Grecian pillars, thus making the protagonist one of Miller's "little men" with stature (if not rank); Golding stages Colley's two-act *sparagmos* as Dionysian theatre. The badger-bag ritual is witnessed by spectators on the quarterdeck, including Summers, Pretti-man, Deverel, Cumbershum, and, of course, Captain Anderson. At the end of the second act, the Dionysian orgy, the sound of the sailors' applause below for Colley's "performance" brings the passengers out on the afterdeck, and the Captain and officers onto the quarterdeck. The crew and the emigrants crowd into the waist, which Talbot calls the pit, and, rightly, since it is they who have the best view, like the groundlings of Shakespeare's time who stood in front of the stage.

Talbot's analogy is as Greek as it is Elizabethan. The ship suggests an amphitheater, like the Theater of Dionysus at Athens or the one at Epidaurus, that slopes downward to the circular orchestra, or in the case of a ship, to the fo'c's'le. The real drama is going on behind the fo'c's'le or, to continue the theatre analogy, behind the Greek *skene* or the Elizabethan arras. It is a drama heard rather than witnessed; like Colley's tragedy, it is a drama without a beginning or a middle but only with an end—a climax in which Colley emerges from the fo'c's'le, supported by Billy—his head resting on the sailor's breast, the drunken Silenus cradled by his Dionysus.

This incomplete drama is microcosmic of the novel in which details must continually be supplied from sources other than the two primary ones. Both acts of the Dionysian drama are incomplete: Talbot never saw the first act because he is with Zenobia during it; Colley never completes his account of the second act because he dies of shame. What drama cannot provide, fiction can.

The Novel as Novel

While Golding's form is tragic, the treatment is novelistic. *Rites of Passage* is the work of a novelist attempting to extend the boundaries of Greek tragedy into fiction and thus transcend their limitations. One of the themes in *Rites of Passage* is the agony of achieving certitude; this is a theme that, while it has been used in film (*Citizen Kane, Rashomon, L'Avventura*) and drama (Pirandello's plays, Ugo Betti's *Queen and the Rebels*), is more satisfactorily explored in the novel where characters function as supplementary channels of information and point of view. While theatre lends itself to the interplay of illusion and reality, that is not Golding's aim. He is not being Pirandellian; he is concerned purely with a reality—a death in need of an explanation. The diarist approach is not the answer; neither is the epistolary, or the theatrical. The novel is; the novel has a long tradition of unreliable narration and multiple point of view. By Henry James's standards, Talbot is unreliable. He did not witness the badger bag; moreover, he would give the story a happy ending by informing Colley's sister that her brother died of a low fever. His epiphanic inference, that Colley died of shame, brings the novel back to its starting point; induction has yielded to deduction.

Possessing the facts, the narrator cannot reach a conclusion; lacking the facts, historians and diarists can only generalize. Chronicle can record, tragedy can dramatize, but the novel can do both—as well as interpret—making it a house of many windows, as Henry James observed. By merging chronicle and tragedy as fiction, Golding can dramatize and interpret Colley's death, using evidence based on Colley's self-characterization in the letter and the testimony of others.

While Talbot was compiling his "who's who" on board, Colley was recording his impressions of the Jolly Tars who "go about their tasks, their bronzed and manly forms unclothed to the waist, their abundant locks gathered in a queue, their nether garments closely fitted but flared about the ankles like the nostrils of a stallion." Just as the novel progresses from the general to the particular, so does Colley's awareness of the tars, beginning with the group and ending with the individual—the Dionysian Billy Rogers, "a narrow-waisted, slim-hipped yet broad-shouldered child of Neptune" (216); a modern Talos filled with liquid fire, some of which Colley will taste.

Colley, who is familiar enough with Greek mythology to know about Talos, proceeds to describe Billy as a Dionysus, never mentioning the fertility god by name (another mark of Golding's irony) but using such language that the identification is unmistakable. Billy is a drinker of wine, a "king" reclining in the bowsprit as if he were in the branches of a tree; perhaps a fir tree, sacred to Dionysus and the kind of tree from which Pentheus was dragged and dismembered. Billy is also a king "crowned with curls," as was Dionysus whose locks so infuriated Pentheus that he had them shorn. That the ship is a Dionysian theater is clear from both the amphitheater imagery and Colley's metonymic description of the ship as a "travelling tree"; the reference harks back to the tree/log/canoe imagery of *The Inheritors* where the tree is a symbol of the Fall, and the canoe made from it brings evil into the world.

Colley's letter serves more than a narrative function; in its Dionysian allusiveness and unabashed homoeroticism it is the voice of Colley's unconscious. If the letter were recast as a stage monologue, it would not have the effect it does embedded in the novel's multilayered narrative. Even Golding's inversion of chronology is in the novelistic tradition. Since the novel is a study in inversion, chronology is not exempt. Golding does not fragment time like a dramatist (e.g., David Hare in *Plenty,* where the play's last scene is, in point of time, the first; Harold Pinter in *Betrayal,* in which the moment an adulterous romance began is dramatized in the final scene, which occurs nine years *before* the opening scene). Instead, Golding uses the familiar convention of the letter, a feature of the epistolary novel, to incorporate events into the narrative that have already taken place in time, but not in the plot. While it may seem that Golding is using Colley's letter for expository purposes, the way Dostoevsky used the letter of Raskolnikov's mother in *Crime and Punishment,* Golding does not introduce the letter until well after the novel's midpoint, and then more as a means of deciphering the writer's past and revealing his present.

Drama could never achieve the simultaneously vertical and horizontal alignment of present and past that comes about in *Rites of Passage.* After *Lord of the Flies,* Golding built his novels on a mythic foundation, from the cellarage to the spire. Each novel contains a primal substratum, an unredeemed world beneath the (so-called) redeemed one, which still bears traces of its primitive past. The foundation in *Rites of Passage* is the hull in which some of the crew have grown a creeper plant, drooping but phallic and emblematic of their own dormant sexuality, which, when revived by Colley's appearance, erupts into an orgy.

The creeper recalls the ivy with which the Bacchants crowned themselves; since ivy grows wild and at random, it fits in naturally with Dionysian worship. The creeper, however, is not the only plant on board; on the quarterdeck there is also Captain Anderson's garland: a leafless plant in the Dionysian hull, a flowering one on the Apollonian quarterdeck. The creeper droops, but the Captain's plant shows signs of blight. The diseased geranium is a powerful metaphor of the pervasiveness of original sin; even if the buds wither above, the vine still grows below. It is as if the white blooms of the geranium were part of the creeper, like white bryony, an evergreen creeper with white flowers with which the Bacchants sometimes garlanded themselves. If the geranium is to be associated with bryony, the symbolism is even more compelling: the exquisite flowers are part of a creeper that must root or cling for support; it is no more possible to separate the blooms from the plant than it is to divorce original sin from human nature, the cellarage from the edifice, or the hull from the quarterdeck. The connecting link is nature.

The Novel as Literary Criticism

Implicit in every literary work is the author's theory of literature. Sometimes it is found in the way the work is constructed and is nothing more than a belief in a plot with a beginning, a middle, and an end, or an insistence that poems have rhyme and meter. Sometimes the work itself constitutes the theory. There is a type of literature—the novel about the writing of a novel, the play about the writing of a play (also the film about the making of a film)—in which whatever the character is writing is the novel we are reading or the play we are seeing. In Sartre's *Nausea*, the diary Roquentin is writing is really the novel *Nausea*; in Jean Anouilh's last play, *Number One*, the protagonist is trying to write a play, which will turn out to be the play we have been watching, as the final scene, which repeats the opening dialogue, proves. Similarly, Talbot's diary and Colley's letter make up the whole of *Rites of Passage*, which is, on one level, a novel about the writing of a journal that evolves into narrative art; on another level, about the means by which that art is achieved.

In *Rites of Passage,* Golding is expounding a theory of literature and art in general by making translation, in the root sense of "passing across," the subsuming metaphor. Translation underlies everything in the novel. The passengers themselves are undergoing translation; they are being carried (transferred) across the sea. As eighteenth-century figures they are products of the great age of translation, translation in the usual sense as "the transference of the content of a text from one language to another."[4] Since the age was so prolific in both theories of translation and translated works for every type of reader (learned ladies, gentlemen, merchants, even the "illiterate" who knew neither Latin nor Greek), it is only natural that the passengers would have more than a passing interest in the subject.

When Miss Granham remarks that "the genius of one language cannot be translated into another," Talbot replies that his godfather, who translated Racine, was said to have improved upon the original. Talbot is not so much talking like Neander in Dryden's *Essay of Dramatic Poesy,* favoring the English over the French, as he is applying the underlying concept of translation to his own circumstances. Talbot was fortunate enough to have a godfather who turned him into an aristocrat just as he turned French alexandrines into English couplets. Colley, on the other hand, is an example of mistranslation; transposed from one class to another, from country parson to divine, he relinquishes his new station to descend into one lower than the first, making a travesty of vertical mobility.

Is there a mean between literal translation and mistranslation? Summers, who balances Talbot's self-aggrandizement and Colley's self-delusion, is also the compromise between the original replicated and the original betrayed. When Summers argues that, in England, it is no more possible for a person to be translated from one class to another than for one language to be translated perfectly into another, Talbot disagrees, citing Summers's own case, the gentleman seaman, as an example. Summers, however, does not regard himself as an example of perfect translation, but of translation "imitating to perfection."

By the use of a single word, "imitating," Golding is able to combine translation with another classical concept, imitation (mimesis, *imitatio*), showing how one is the natural outgrowth of the other. If translation imitates the original, it can be said to represent or mirror it, keeping its essence intact while changing only the accidents. Thus the best translations may omit words but never ideas.

Understood in this way, *Rites of Passage* is also about literature classically conceived as an imitation of life, a mirror of nature. But what sort of imitation? Literal or free? Or, to use Dryden's terms, metaphrase ("word by word, line by line") or paraphrase ("translation with latitude"). And what sort of mirror—magnifying, minimizing, or distorting? The first indication that the novel is, among other things, about literature occurs when Talbot decides he will be selective in what he records. Selectivity is indispensable to mimesis, which requires the portrayal only of what is representative and what is abiding in human nature instead of what is particular and transitory.

Talbot does not understand human nature. If everyone were of his class, or rather of the class to which patronage has raised him, he might be able to tell a story with universality. But he cannot tell Colley's story; the letter clashes with the journal in every conceivable way—stylistically, morally, aesthetically. Thus Talbot has no other choice but to incorporate it verbatim, as if it were a source to be cited. There is another reason why he cannot tell Colley's story: Talbot has no sympathy for the clergyman because, according to Talbot's reading of Aristotle, Colley is not wellborn and therefore is an unsuitable subject for tragedy. Talbot is a victim of the medieval misconception of the *Poetics* in which rank is never given as a requirement for tragedy; Aristotle wrote that the tragic protagonist must be well known, not wellborn.

While there are two writers in *Rites of Passage,* there is one author: William Golding who, by assigning the narrative to his characters, can retire behind the scenes and create what they write about. As the unseen author, he can also give each account a subtext that grows deeper with each turn of events, thus revealing how fiction in the highest sense of the word results when feeling, reason, and imagination—the conscious and unconscious—interpenetrate. Golding does what neither narrator can do: he makes their accounts converge on a metaphorical level, since each can only proceed on a literal one. By giving the major part of the narration to Talbot, Golding is subtly criticizing narrative that is all rhetoric and no feeling. Talbot is an excellent stylist, as he is not above telling his godfather; but he is a superficial storyteller with a gift only for the theatrical. In an earlier age, he might have been a minor Restoration playwright. He is impatient with trivial (or Richardsonian) details, yet he records, however grandly, a plethora of trivia. His desire for the nautical *mot juste* causes him to revel in

"Tarpaulin language." His self-indulgence results in his missing significant events; whatever is important he learns from others. If one
remembers that the voyage is far from over by the time his journal
ends, it is amazing how little he has actually recorded. A man has died
from degradation; those who seemed to be one thing turned out to be
another; Talbot's own servant may have been killed because, in the
tradition of detective fiction, he may have known too much; a new
order is beginning; and Talbot puts away his journal, planning to sew
it up in sailcloth and lock it away. All he has learned is that "men can
die of shame."

Talbot's deficiencies as a narrator can ultimately be traced to his
misunderstanding of mimesis, the cornerstone of classical art, which
he should know, as one who quotes Greek. When he discovers that
Brocklebank has painted a famous picture of Lord Nelson's death, he
remarks that it is inaccurate; Nelson was depicted as dying in the presence of his grieving officers while, in truth, he died alone. Although
Brocklebank is drunk, he is able to explain to the educated Talbot that
the classical doctrine of verisimilitude does not demand the unvar-
nished truth but the semblance of truth; not truth as it is but as it
should be. Thus a painter may make a sloop a frigate, or a solitary
death a spectacle.

This is precisely how the ancients approached historiography. The
funeral oration that Pericles delivers in Thucydides' *History of the Pel-
oponnesian War* is a fabrication; it is what, according to Thucydides,
Pericles ought to have said under the best of circumstances, not what
he actually said; it is the speech Pericles would have delivered if he had
had Thucydides' verbal gifts. Talbot does not understand the basic difference between history and tragedy, between the nonmimetic and the
mimetic. History portrays the particular, tragedy the universal; history, what did happen; tragedy, what could happen.

Talbot is a chronicler, not a tragedian. If he ever reworked Colley's
letter into his journal, it would have been something like the *Oedipus*
of John Dryden and Nathaniel Lee—quaintly melodramatic and a bit
ludicrous. If Colley were ever to read it, he would no more understand
Talbot's account than Dionysus would understand Apollo. As narrators, Talbot and Colley are as different from each other as the Augus-
tans were from the romantics.

This is Golding's thesis: the rites of passage the passengers are
undergoing are of various kinds: tribal, social, linguistic, literary. Like

Darkness Visible, Rites of Passage is also about language—the choice of words, the proper way of expressing ideas. Language, like England, is changing; if the ship symbolizes Britain, the novel reflects the changes occurring in British society. A new class is emerging, a new middle class that will not observe the eighteenth-century laws of decorum or believe in the primacy of wit; it is a class that will believe in the superiority of feeling, having never learned to speak in the idiom of the coffee house or the salon. Colley writes with a Wordsworthian simplicity and directness, which is particularly apparent at the end of his letter when he looks out at the sea: "I gazed down into the water, the blue, the green, the purple, the snowy, sliding foam! I saw with a new feeling of security the long green weed that wavers under the water from our wooden sides" (247).

Coming from the country—which in the Preface to Second Edition of the *Lyrical Ballads* (1800) Wordsworth claims is superior to the city because it affords glimpses into the universal—Colley approximates Wordsworth's ideal: a common person living close to nature. That a new era is dawning is also evident in the way Golding works Coleridge into the novel—by making Brocklebank a painter of his portrait. Talbot is vaguely aware of Coleridge, but the significance of the *Lyrical Ballads* eludes him; he does not seem to know "The Rime of the Ancient Mariner," which was included in the 1798 edition of the *Lyrical Ballads*. Yet Zenobia the prostitute knows it and can even quote from it. Coleridge is the poet of the new order, the author of a poem that a whore can understand; and Coleridge's albatross has become so familiar that the freethinker Prettiman vows to shoot one, merely to prove he is free of superstition. What is genuinely tragic about Colley, apart from his lack of self-knowledge, is his ignorance of his literary heritage: he was one of the first romantics.

In *Rites of Passage,* one can appreciate the distance Golding has come since *Lord of the Flies.* Always preoccupied with Dionysus, without whom tragedy would never have evolved beyond ritual, he is now able to see how the spirit of Dionysus dominates history. Since the god represents the life force, that force will be continually felt—more strongly at some times than at others, and most strongly when a rationally conceived world is about to yield to a world of feeling. This is, after all, how the worship of Dionysus originated in Greece; threatened by the arrival of the new god, Apollo had to accommodate him. At first, accommodation was tokenism; in alternate years, during midwinter when the oracle of Apollo was not functioning, Dionysian worship was allowed. But the god proved too powerful; he was no more able to be contained by a calendar than by the march of events. By translating Dionysus from tragedy into historical fiction, Golding has accomplished what none of his characters could: a perfect Drydenian paraphrase.

Chapter Eleven
Impurely Academic
A Writer's Vengeance

William Golding owes much to academe. Through ingenious market-
ing and the willingness of college instructors to adopt *Lord of the Flies*
in Introduction to Literature courses, Golding entered the English curriculum in the 1960s; shortly afterward, he entered the English major.
His fifth novel had no sooner appeared than he was the subject of a
monograph. Although Golding has always been dubious of the academy, he must surely realize that he could never have reached his present
stature if he had not first been the subject of study and then the object
of criticism. Unlike Joyce Carol Oates, whose response to a negative
review used to be a letter to the editor, Golding has refrained from
such exchanges. Reviewers do not bother him as much as academics;
he can shrug off reviewers ("They didn't like that one," he once remarked nonchalantly of *Free Fall*). Academics, however, are another
matter; he was once one of them. When he left Oxford in 1935, it was
with a B.A. in English and a diploma in education. Later he accepted
a position at Bishop Wordsworth's School, a public school in Salisbury
where, except for the five years he spent in the Royal Navy during
World War II, he remained until 1962. Although Golding is affected
by the judgment of academics, he also knows that, unlike hardened
reviewers, they are vulnerable and thus deflatable. This is especially
true of English professors; they lend themselves to parody because they
are halved creatures, thinking that they teach a subject (literature)
while they are really analyzing an object (a text); they consider themselves teachers while they are really interpreters, or as Plato would say,
interpreters of interpreters.

Since Golding knows that academics can misinterpret a text as well
as interpret it, he is suspicious of them. While he grants them interviews and, in one instance, cooperated in a book-length interview, he
tends to be disdainful of them, perhaps because he feels he can do for
himself what academics have done for him, and maybe even do it better: that is, explicate his work, as he has done in interviews, addresses,

and lectures. Teachers come off badly in Golding; they are pedantic, unfeeling, or so neurotic that their neuroses carry over into the classroom, impeding the exchange of knowledge that should be taking place.

What particularly bothers Golding is the gulf between morality and learning, a gulf that is widened when teachers are unable to impart a moral dimension to education. In the case of the humanities, this failure is disastrous; the result is not so much disinterested knowledge, which is bad enough, as textbook knowledge that is totally divorced from a moral or even a personal context. During his American lecture tour in the early 1960s, he witnessed a class in creative writing in which the students and instructor bandied about such terms as "sex image," "superego," and "id"; and a sensitive youth was told to recast his poem as a sonnet with questions in the octet and answers in the sestet.[1]

Golding's distrust of the academy increased during the 1970s as his reputation waned; however, when he reestablished himself with *Darkness Visible* and *Rites of Passage,* the distrust exploded into revenge in 1983, the year he became Nobel laureate and wrote *The Paper Men.* In one way, *The Paper Men* is an affront to those who had, indirectly at least, contributed to his winning the prize by teaching his works, and by writing about them at a time when they had fallen into desuetude. Thus *The Paper Men* seems like misdirected revenge, even if one realizes that the revenge is also self-directed since it reflects, to some extent, self-hatred. The novelist in *The Paper Men* is a thinly disguised persona for Golding and not much better than the English professor who relentlessly pursues him.

Self and Shadow

The situation was promising and might have worked if Golding had been Nabokov. The atmosphere is Nabokovian, and while Golding makes allusions to Ibsen, Shakespeare, and Virgil, he makes only one to Vladimir Nabokov, and that is to the brief period the narrator, Sir Wilfred Barclay, spends as an itinerant lecturer, finding himself at one point in "Nabokov country"—an allusion to Nabokov's teaching stints at Wellesley and Cornell in the 1940s and 1950s.[2] In *Lolita,* Nabokov created the most intriguing set of doubles in contemporary literature: Humbert Humbert and Clare Quilty, Humbert's dark side, his shadow, who pursues Humbert and Lolita on their cross-country trips, appearing in the most unlikely places and in the most unlikely disguises (e.g., a spinster); similarly, in *The Paper Men*, Rick L. Tucker, Assistant Professor of English, pursues renowned novelist Wilfred Barclay for fourteen years, popping up in Seville, Hamburg, Spurli, and perhaps even Marrakesh. While Quilty is characterized in terms of apelike imagery, Tucker has the qualities of a dog; at one point Barclay reduces his shadow to canine fury by making him drink wine from a saucer.

Significantly, Tucker makes his first appearance as a badger and is, appropriately, bagged; his subsequent humiliation, while reminiscent of Colley's during the badger bag, is more demeaning than debasing. In an effort to achieve immortality by attaching himself to an immortal, Tucker, while still a graduate student, insinuates himself into Barclay's favors, as well as into his household, by posing as an assistant professor of English eager to do a critical study of Barclay's fiction. Tucker has taken his course in Methods of Literary Scholarship seriously; anxious to locate primary sources, he rifles the Barclays' garbage can, causing his host to mistake him for a badger and shoot him with an airgun. The wound is superficial, as befits Tucker; the real wounds, however, are suffered by Barclay whose letter to a former mistress, discarded among the garbage, comes to light, prompting his wife to divorce him.

Just as the plot seems to take wing, the wings turn out to be Icarian; they sustain the narrative only for a moment and then melt, leaving Golding in an auctorial pose, playing with the reader as Barclay played with Tucker and writing a novel that turns out to be the authorized biography that Tucker was burning to do. *The Paper Men* could have been a study in spiraling irony, a mode for which Golding is temperamentally and stylistically suited. Ironies not only abound; they multiply. In Switzerland, Tucker supposedly saves Barclay from falling to his death; as it turns out, there was a meadow below that would have broken the fall anyway. Doubting the stigmata of Padre Pio, the mystic, Barclay ends up receiving the stigmata himself. The final irony is that, just as there seems to be a possibility of reconciliation between Barclay and his wife, he returns to find her dying of cancer and cursing him for his selfishness.

Unfortunately, Golding cannot sustain the irony; the novel is such a personal vendetta against academe that the author's vengeful glee results in inconsistency and carelessness. Barclay is not university educated, yet for one who has never gone beyond the fifth, he has, like Golding, a command of the classics; his language is studded with Latin phrases, he makes allusions to Virgil's *Eclogues* and Longus's *Daphnis and Chloe* (not exactly fifth-form reading), and uses expressions like *ithyphallic* and *Gaia Mater.*

Furthermore, Golding's perception of American higher education and American literary scholarship is, at best, superficial; at worst, inaccurate. Tucker is a type with whom most living writers, including Golding, are familiar: the parasitic graduate student or the unpublished assistant professor anxious to "do" an unmined author for reasons ranging anywhere from an easy dissertation topic to tenure and promotion to ego gratification and reflected glory. Tucker is precisely that—a type. While he may be typical of a limited species, he is not typical of the American professor, any more than Eve Harrington in the film *All about Eve* is typical of a stage actress. Both Eve and Tucker attempt to achieve fame by insinuating themselves into the lives of the famous. At least in the film, Joseph L. Mankiewicz supplied Eve with a plausible background; the background Golding has provided for Tucker does not ring true, no matter how hard one tries to suspend disbelief. Tucker's vita reads like bad satire; first he is a graduate student, then an assistant professor in the Department of English and Allied Studies at the University of Astrakhan in Nebraska, sporting a pullover with "Ole Ashcan" inscribed on it. The inscription may reflect Golding's view of the American university or his misconception of Ole Miss. Still, it is a bad pun as well as an improbable one; while a university's name might lend itself to parody, it is difficult to imagine its encouraging self-deprecation with parodistic clothing.

Wooing the Cankered Muse

There are few things sadder than satire that falls flat because of overconfidence; when humor is deliberately programmed to get a laugh, it frequently deprograms itself into deadly silence. Such is the case with Mrs. Tucker's major: flower-arranging and bibliography, a tired variation on the old joke about the basket-weaving major at Easy-A U.

Apart from humor that backfires, there are implausibilities that mount. Golding, who has little use for linguistics, makes Tucker a practitioner of that discipline. Yet why a teacher of linguistics and phonetics would latch on to a novelist, and not to a Chomsky or an Eco, is unclear. Furthermore, while there are certain similarities (but more differences) between William Golding and Wilfred Barclay, one must accept the latter's celebrity on faith. If *The Paper Men* is any indication of Barclay's talent, it exists only in an inchoate form; the writer may be gifted, but he is also solipsistic, self-indulgent, and self-enraptured—traits that William Golding does not appear to share. While one can understand an academic's pursuing William Golding, it is hard to imagine anyone's pursuing Wilfred Barclay. There might be some humor in a linguist's venturing into the deeper waters of literary biography, but Golding repeats the stock clichés about the field by having Tucker deliver a paper on the frequency of the relative clause in Barclay's fiction.

Although satire is not intended to be taken literally, Golding has incorporated it into a plot that, on one level, demands to be taken literally since it comprises the last twenty years of Barclay's life. Golding is too meticulous a craftsman to neglect structure, even though he may be indifferent to details. To provide a chronological framework for the narrative he arranges a ten-year hiatus between the time Tucker was a scavenging houseguest and a full-fledged academic on sabbatical. The chronology, however, has been forced on the narrative because Golding is trying to have it both ways: he is portraying an academic opportunist, but for that portrayal to be valid, the academic should at least be typical of the academy. Tucker is typical of a type—the academic groupie. By making Tucker a graduate student when he first meets Barclay, Golding expects us to believe that Tucker finished his degree, found a position, and after seven years won tenure and a sabbatical. While tenure is often bestowed on unworthy recipients, it is hard to imagine Tucker's lasting anywhere, even at Ole Ashcan, for seven years unless, true to its name, the school honored detritus.

Why Tucker's sabbatical did not coincide with a promotion to associate professor, as it ordinarily does, may be attributable to Golding's faulty knowledge of American university practice. At any rate, the sabbatical is a plot peg to engineer a second meeting between the men. Since Golding has made Tucker a dark alter ego, he must get Tucker out of the classroom and onto the continent so he can track Barclay. Thus he must invent an explanation: a sabbatical. Nabokov did not have to invent an explanation for Quilty's turning up during the two cross-country trips that Humbert and Lolita take. Nabokov was not writing a realistic novel; Golding is using the conventions of realism (motivation, narrative links, geographical detail). Since the novel spans twenty years, Golding must provide another explanation for Tucker's roaming around Europe when he should be teaching the phonetic alphabet. This explanation is the weakest of the lot: Tucker is being subsidized by a philanthropist, known only as Halliday, who has given him seven years to write a biography of Barclay because Halliday "collects" authors and believes, in some Mephistophelian way, that having their biography is equivalent to possessing their soul.

It all seems so bizarre that one is tempted to conclude that Tucker is mad, Barclay is hallucinating, and Halliday is nonexistent. Barclay's stock response, "ha et cetera," makes one wonder if Halliday does not personify that response and is just a laugh. If so, the laugh is on the reader. More likely, Halliday is Golding's symbol of the unseen presence behind the academic establishment; the plutocrat who endows chairs and has scholarships and buildings named after him, but always with strings attached. If Tucker had been a research scientist and Barclay a Nobel laureate in physics, Halliday's largesse might have made sense. But why would anyone pay for a biography of Wilfred Barclay? Since Golding may have sensed that Halliday's satanic mania for possession is not especially compelling, he comes up with another reason: Halliday's interest in Tucker's wife, but this may explain the subsidy, not the biography.

What Golding would like to imply is that behind Tucker's dogged perseverance is something even more frightening, perhaps more evil: a force able to perpetuate mediocrity by subsidizing it. If Tucker were an Iago and Halliday a Mephistopheles, Golding's thesis would hold; but neither is. Even when Tucker kills Barclay at the end, it is more out of frustration than malevolence. Thus the entire novel is reduced to a maxim: novelists should leave nothing for posterity but their works. For just before Tucker fires his bullet, Barclay burns everything but the manuscript that, if the conceit is pushed to its obvious conclusion, is what we have just been reading: *The Paper Men.*

The difficulty with *The Paper Men* is that Golding came to it fresh from his triumph in *Rites of Passage;* there, he was able to work motifs and devices that had become his hallmark (doubles, prey as predator) into a fiction that was the combined narratives of two characters. He tried to do something similar in *The Paper Men,* this time making the novel the narrative of his own persona, so that at the end the real self would separate from the fictive self, and the message would be heard loud and clear: life and work, work and criticism, criticism and art, art and life are and must always be distinct. Yet it did not work; the termini had been widened so much that complete bipolarity results. Barclay and Golding are at such opposite extremes—as are Tucker and the American academic, Ole Ashcan and the American university, Hal-

liday and American philanthropy—that whatever correspondences exist are obscured by the differences. Moreover, Apollo and Dionysus
have moved to opposite ends of the pantheon. There are no more bla-
tant opposites in Golding than Tucker and Barclay—the former, a parody of the Apollonian; the latter, a travesty of the Dionysian. Jack and
Ralph are normal by comparison. The saddest aspect of *The Paper Men*
is the persona Golding has adopted. It is too thin for the person; Golding keeps protruding from it. Perhaps Barclay is what Golding might
have become if he had been a philanderer or a rotter. To say that the
author is more substantial than his fictional counterpart may be flat-
tering to the author as a person, but it is damning to the author as
novelist.

Invention and Selection

In the classical tradition, invention (*inventio*) is a rhetorical term
denoting the process of finding the arguments for a speech. The same
notion is applicable to fiction where the writer must "find" his or her
subject matter, delimiting it and choosing only what is representative
and universal. Selection, then, is implicit in invention; taken together,
they constitute the basis of writing and of art.

In *The Paper Men,* Golding continues to explore the subject of artistic selection that was so well illustrated in *Rites of Passage*. That the
narrator of *The Paper Men* is a novelist, as opposed to the diarist and
letter-writer in *Rites of Passage,* should have enabled Golding to argue
even more forcefully that art requires choices but that before they can
be made, the artist must "discover" the subject matter. Barclay, unfortunately, is incapable of invention: "No more invention, only selection." Since the two are inseparable, he cannot accomplish the second
goal until he achieves the first; if he invents ("finds") his material, he
can select. But because he cannot invent, he cannot select. What Barclay "finds" is a sort of found object, a circular situation in which a
critic preys on a writer who in turn preys on the critic who kills the
writer who is writing the book that we are reading. While Barclay
vows only to select, what he has selected hardly seems typical of either
predator or prey. There are too many narrative gaps, too many breaches
of verisimilitude, too many jumps in time, too many unanswered questions about the reality or illusiveness of some of the incidents. After a
while, it does not seem to matter whether or not Tucker saw Barclay
in Marrakesh.

For the second time, *Free Fall* being the first, Golding has strayed into unfamiliar territory. While he understands the techniques of the eighteenth-century novel, he cannot make them work in a modern setting that is alien to him and in a world for which he has little sympathy. In *Darkness Visible,* Golding had allegory to sustain him; in *The Paper Men,* he has only his faith in God as he wades through the marshes of postmodernism, sinking into the bogs made by novels that were really diaries, self-begetting novels, fictions that were fabulations, and fabulations that never became fiction—the flotsam created by invention turned against itself. In the past, Golding never worried about ellipses; the reader had to fill them in. In *The Paper Men,* Barclay justifies narrative lacunae, apologizing for incomplete portraits by the fact that he has lost his notes or cannot go beyond what he has sketched. Given his random existence, his excessive drinking, and his self-loathing, Barclay would find it hard to select, even harder to invent. What is burned at the end may have been more interesting than what is retained.

Golding is one of the few contemporary writers who affirms a belief in God and, to prove it, writes a novel in which a believing writer comes off badly. Moreover, the writer has some affinity with the author. Golding intended an association between himself and Barclay; it may be a tenuous one, a "there but by the grace of God go I" one, but it is still an association. Since Barclay is Golding's creation as well as his shadow self, Golding punishes both himself and his character.

Barclay is the sort who thrives on humiliating others. When he discovers Tucker in his pyjamas rummaging through the garbage, he too is in pyjamas. When Barclay's bottoms fall down, he feels the need to degrade Tucker; after wounding him, he tries to find the wound and in the process exposes Tucker's "shaggy privates." The incident delights Barclay, whose sadism is almost infantile; it is as if Barclay were a public school prefect and Tucker a fag to be degraded at will. Tucker's privates, indeed his simian body, fascinate Barclay; his fascination is not erotic, since Barclay loathes homosexuals, but anthropological. To Barclay, Tucker is an anthropoid or at least nonhuman. Thus, when he tempts Tucker with the prospect of being his official biographer, Barclay reduces him to canine subservience, making him drink wine from a saucer. At first Tucker complies, but when he realizes the state to which he has been reduced, he retaliates, striking Barclay in anger.

Barclay's suffering is only beginning. On one of the Lipari Islands, in a world half pagan and half Christian (the kind Golding knows

best), Barclay suffers a stroke. The circumstances leading to it are unusual—for Barclay, at least. In a church he sees a silver Christ, whose
metal evokes a response within himself. The realization that his soul is
as metallic as the statue induces a stroke. Providence punishes Barclay
(with Golding's sanction), but Golding punishes himself. If Wilfred
Barclay is taken as a partial as well as an anti-self-portrait, it is easy to
see that the author is administering a double penance, inflicting pain
on his character as well as on himself for writing a petty novel—one
that is neither satire, which is usually instructive, or parody, which is
usually playful, but merely a display of vindictiveness.

Golding, whose aversion to homosexuality led him to portray homosexuals satirically, condescendingly, and only in one instance sympathetically (Pedigree in *Darkness Visible*), allows a homosexual writer
to describe Barclay as a man with an exoskeletal soul and a carapace for
flesh; in short, a moral lobster. As such, he is brother to Pincher Martin, who was also grasping and incapable of touch. Golding has not let
himself off the hook; if there is a bit of Barclay in him, there is also a
modicum of Martin.

A Sad Summary

Ultimately, what is defeating about *The Paper Men* is its summary
nature: the novel is a reliquary of former themes and motifs. Perhaps
Golding thought *Rites of Passage* had not done the job and needed an
appendix. Yet the themes worked better in earlier novels: the prey-
predator dichotomy and synonymy in *Lord of the Flies*, the fall in *The
Inheritors*, the lobster metaphor in *Pincher Martin*. The interchangeable
hunter and hunted in *Lord of the Flies* grew out of a situation in which
the hunters were hounded by drives and fears they did not understand,
making them the prey of the predator within. To portray the age-old
conflict between the academic critic and the creative writer in such
terms, turning it into an anthropological passion play, credits the critic
with supernatural powers and academe with a native mythology. The
fall was a far richer symbol in *The Inheritors* where it derived from the
waterfall; the waterfall in *The Paper Men* is part of the Alpine landscape,
and the fall is just a tumble. The lobster metaphor succeeded in *Pincher
Martin* because the lobster claws in the pit on Rockall were a reminder
of the transformations and purgations those who allow their souls to
petrify undergo. Calling Barclay a spiritual crustacean is just a little

more vivid than calling him a moral monster, but the difference is one of degree, not kind. Golding was never as successful in handling doubles as he was in *Rites of Passage*. A voyage is conducive to the creation of mirror images; a twenty-year odyssey, in which the doubles are not always together, is not.

While the novel's premise—writer and critic as alter egos—is ingenious, the coinciding of personalities can only succeed if they are similar. In Shaw's *Pygmalion*, Henry Higgins and Eliza Doolittle are doubles in several senses. Although each is the social reverse of the other, each has personality traits of the other. More important, Higgins and Eliza are equally intelligent, but in different ways. The climactic moment in the film *True Grit* occurs when Rooster Cogburn (John Wayne) realizes how similar Mattie (Kim Darby) is to himself: "She reminds me of me," he exclaims.

Tucker is only vaguely reminiscent of Barclay, and vice versa. They only seem to have two features in common: they use people, especially women, although Barclay is more subtle about it than Tucker; and each brings out the beast in the other. Barclay reduces Tucker to a dog; in his canine role, Tucker leaps on Barclay in his club and bites him. Tucker also brings out the dog in Barclay, who often behaves like one, even to the point of saying "yap yap." Although their relationship is sadistically and masochistically reciprocal, Barclay pays the greater price; Tucker has brought out traits in him that make him a mediocre human being and prevent his writing a worthy book, just as an animus against academe has done the same to Golding.

Neither figure is up to par. If the novel we have been reading is the biography Barclay will offer Tucker, *The Paper Men* must be judged as Barclay's, as well as Golding's, work. It is the work of a writer who has had a bad day, a writer capable of brilliant and moving passages but who has not been able to reconcile fact and fiction, invention and selection. Tucker, on the other hand, is incapable of anything: teaching, criticism, or scholarship.

Tucker lacks Barclay's one redeeming quality: guilt. In his dreams, whether nightmarish or paradisal, Barclay punishes himself. Once he dreams he is treading burning sands, a strange fate reminiscent of the sodomites in the *Inferno* who must walk ceaselessly across a burning plain. Barclay is unconsciously punishing himself for his homophobia; although he would deny it, he subjects Tucker to humiliation—a motif found in homosexual drama, expressed both overtly (Mart Crowley's

Boys in the Band) and in disguised form (Anthony Shaffer's *Sleuth*); in each, one male subjects another to ritual degradation, which is what happens in *The Paper Men*.

In another dream, Barclay seems to be in paradise, but it turns out to be hell. Halliday, whom Barclay equates with the demonic power behind academe, and Rome's Spanish Stairs, which he considers a gathering place for misfits, blend into a Dantean phantasmagoria with Halliday as Barclay's Beatrice and the Spanish Stairs as the stairway to heaven. But instead of hearing the music of the spheres, as Dante does in the *Paradiso* (canto 1), Barclay hears the sound of guitars, characteristic music of the 1960s, which he abominates. The new elect are not saints but flower children; the sexual differences that made it possible for Barclay to enjoy women have been blurred into androgyny. Heaven has become hell, the ultimate penance because it is the ultimate inversion.

The novel that began with Barclay's shooting Tucker with an airgun comes full circle with Tucker's shooting Barclay with a rifle. The shadow self survives the true self; the damned survives the regenerate; and, horror of horrors, the academic survives the writer. Whatever Barclay may lack, he at least has self-knowledge, which sets him poles apart from Tucker. Lying in a hospital bed after his stroke, he is forced to practice separate syllables. Wanting to say "end," he says "sin" instead; trying again, he says: "Not. Sin. I. am. sin" (127). Taken together, the words form the great paradox of Christianity: humankind, whose end is to know God, accomplishes that end through sin—original sin, which, once committed, must be atoned for. Thus it is only through sin and an understanding of the Fall that humankind knows God. This knowledge with its awesome implications is something Tucker could never comprehend, despite his doctorate. But then, Tucker has only read Wilfred Barclay, not William Golding.

Chapter Twelve
The Making of a Nobel Prize Winner

Dark Horse Visible

When William Golding was awarded the Nobel Prize for literature in October 1983, even his staunchest admirers were surprised. If a Briton were to be honored, Graham Greene, a frequent contender, would have seemed the logical choice; more likely, speculators argued, the award would go to a woman—Marguerite Yourcenar or Nadine Gordimer. Golding did not even appear to be a dark horse. Although the choice seemed eccentric to some and unwise to others, Golding was at least a familiar name—something Nobel laureates have not always been. When Golding won, the question was not "who?" as it was with Vicente Aleixandre in 1977 or Czeslaw Milosz in 1980, but "why?" Strangely enough, that question was not raised in 1978 when the Swedish Academy honored another popular writer, Isaac Bashevis Singer; but it was with Golding. In what was clearly a breach of etiquette, poet-critic Artur Lundkvist, who had been championing French novelist Claude Simon, deplored the Academy's decision, calling Golding a "decent" writer but undeserving of such distinction.[1]

As it happened, Lundkvist"s violation of secrecy prompted an interesting disclosure from the academy: Golding had been under consideration for three years. Thus he had become a potential candidate after publishing *Darkness Visible,* which marked his return to fiction. *Rites of Passage* and a second book of essays, *A Moving Target,* which soon followed, confirmed Golding's literary comeback. The latter revealed that Golding was more aware of contemporary developments, in literature and elsewhere, than had previously been believed.

Golding had now become critically respectable, a *literatus* if not a man of letters. He had not just a few books but an oeuvre that could be viewed as a continuous exploration of two major themes in contemporary literature: freedom and evil. Instead of being stymied by existentialist antinarrative, Golding found his metier in fiction that was multileveled yet accessible to a broad readership. Golding's popularity was clearly a factor in his receiving the Nobel Prize, as the academy acknowledged in its citation: "William Golding's novels and stories are not only somber moralities and dark myths about evil and treacherous and destructive forces. They are also colorful tales of adventure which can be read as such, full of narrative joy, inventiveness and excitement."[2]

Although Golding's detractors found the award ironic, the real irony occurred the next day when Golding received a parking ticket. When he offered to pay the fine immediately, he was told by a bureaucratic policeman to fill out the envelope in which the ticket was enclosed, make out a check for the exact amount, address the envelope correctly, put a stamp on it, and mail it. Then the officer added: "And may we congratulate you on winning the Nobel Prize for Literature."[3] Golding chose to end his Nobel lecture with this anecdote. Nothing has done more to cultivate Golding's ironic sense than his own career, which began with a novel that became a cause célèbre, but one whose initial reviews were only cautious or moderately favorable, no barometer of the wave of popular acceptance that would soon engulf it. Since then *Lord of the Flies* has occasioned a case book, two American study guides, two British study guides (infinitely better), and a plethora of articles claiming analogues from Freud to *Peter Pan*.[4] During the 1960s, *Lord of the Flies* was required reading for political science majors, used to illustrate the antipastoral, and assigned to Peace Corps volunteers to learn about "the essential conflicts between man's individual well being and the rules of society."[5]

Then the tide began to turn. Some of the academics who used *Lord of the Flies* to introduce their students to serious literature turned on Golding, branding the novel "fool's gold": "What is of primary importance is that Golding has used a delicate subject . . . and that thousands of readers have been used in their turn."[6] In this connection, Kenneth Rexroth's opinion is worth noting, if for no other reason than its snideness: "Like Salinger, Golding is one of those authors schoolteachers say all the young read. It's easy to see how this works out. They say to their classes as they assign *Catcher in the Rye* or *Lord of the Flies,* 'You have to read this book.' . . . So they did with my daughter. 'How did you like *Catcher in the Rye?*' 'Not much,' she said. Later, 'How did you like *Lord of the Flies?*' 'I can't read it.' Maybe she was just raised right."[7]

Regardless, *Lord of the Flies* was a publishing and a pedagogical phenomenon; its rise from a book that went out of print soon after its American publication in 1955 to a paperback bestseller by 1962 would constitute a study in itself. John Peter's article, the first American essay to take a serious look at Golding, appeared in the 1957 *Kenyon Review*. A paperback edition, complete with a biographical sketch and an essay for the uninitiated, was published two years later. In November 1961, Golding's nonfiction began to appear, starting in *Holiday*. He spent a year as a rarely resident writer-in-residence (1961–62) at Hollins College; at the same time he embarked on an American lecture tour that took him to Harvard, Vassar, Dartmouth, the Choate School, and the University of Pennsylvania; he even ended up on the *Today* show where, bleary-eyed, he answered questions about Simon's being a Christ-figure.

Regardless of the hype, *Lord of the Flies* is still an impressive novel, and it would be hard to find one as good from any other post–World War II novelist. Iris Murdoch, with whom Golding is sometimes paired as a writer of moral concerns (*The Bell* is a good companion piece to *The Spire*), also began her career in 1954 with *Under the Net*, an academic exercise (and teachable) that is somewhere between a picaresque novel and a bildungsroman, but is really neither and only hints at what she would later accomplish.

There is, however, a major difference between Murdoch and Golding: Murdoch was never a freshman English text; when she entered the English curriculum, it was through the Modern British Novel or Contemporary Fiction courses. Although she may have repeated herself, and has been accused of doing so, her reputation never really declined; it only waxed and waned because it had not peaked. Golding's had; in 1964, with *The Spire,* he had become the Aeschylean novelist he hoped to be: one who probed moral conflicts and was no more satisfied with a surface examination than Aeschylus was.

Nineteen sixty-four was a year of peace in the United States; while it cannot be likened to 1941, it was still one of those end-of-innocence years, the year before the escalation of the Vietnam war. As the United States sank into the quagmire of an undeclared war in Southeast Asia, a generation arose that was unwilling to accept evil as inevitable and human nature as intrinsically flawed. And so, *Lord of the Rings* replaced *Lord of the Flies;* Hesse's *Steppenwolf* and Kesey's *One Flew over the Cuckoo's Nest*, with their unthreatening profundity, edged *Lord of the Flies* out of the introductory literature course. Woodstock nation rejected *Lord of the Flies* because "it no longer suits the temper of the times" and "readers today do not accept the moral of the fable because it contradicts their faith in social manipulation."[8] As original sin fell out of fashion, so did Golding. While *The Pyramid* pointed to a change of vision, the reviews did not encourage anyone to notice it. If *Lord of the Flies* lost its popularity during the Vietnam war, it may be because the young would not accept its tragic view of humankind and because the novel "seems to deny them what they claim as their birthright: easy hopes, commitment to democratic ideals and beneficient transformations in society; in short, a fulfillment of their ardent dream of the sweetness and light to prevail after the current 'revolution.'"[9]

If *Lord of the Flies* had entered the canon in a more conventional way, through articles and papers and not as a replacement for *The Catcher in the Rye*, it might have escaped the vicissitudes of syllabus revision. Teachers are always looking for the ideal Introduction to Literature novel. In the mid 1950s, it was J. D. Salinger's novel, which blended in well with crewcuts and white bucks, pony tails and penny loafers. Those who taught it had probably first read it under the bedcovers with a flashlight.

But by the end of the 1950s, the sons and daughters of Holden Caulfield were no longer moonstruck idealists eager to cleanse lavatory walls of obscenities; there were too many walls, too many obscenities. Those who went on to become teachers wanted to do for their students what their teachers had done for them: introduce them to something contemporary rather than to the traditional Victorian novel. "The age demanded" a successor to *Catcher*, which then entered secondary school (as *Lord of the Flies* would) where its literary value was often eclipsed by the number of dismissals it occasioned.

The requirements for *Catcher*'s replacement were: that it should be about adolescents who are not yet collegians; it should be well written and contain figurative language, ambivalence, symbolism that was natural rather than private, foreshadowing, and empathetic characters; above all, it should be teachable. While some instructors preferred John Knowles's *Separate Peace*, most agreed that *Lord of the Flies* fulfilled the requirements admirably. In addition, there was just enough of the exotic in the plot to attract those who remembered the last days of the movie serial or who saw the early installments of *Ramar of the Jungle* on television. *Lord of the Flies* straddled the end of adolescence and the beginning of adulthood; it was, in short, the perfect book for an eighteen-year-old.

From Classic to Kiddie Lit

Then came Vietnam; the shadow it cast was larger than the dirty war it was. Like some infernal machine, the war fed on America's problems (race, the draft, campus unrest, social injustice) and spewed them out in uglier form. Golding's polarized universe was unpalatable to student militants and their sympathizers; his was the kind of world they were trying to change. Tolkien with his benign way of storytelling was preferable; he sugarcoated the pill of life, making it easier to swallow. For those in search of a more searing humanity, there was Hesse. Meanwhile, Golding's minor classic, which had gone from being one of the most rejected books in the history of publishing to a required text, moved down into the high schools, then to junior high. If Golding is distrustful of academics, it is with good reason; he was the victim of one of the most insidious games in the profession—the quest for a new and relevant author who could be dissected in the classroom and then discarded like a mutilated cadaver when nothing examinable was left. Golding had become one of his own scapegoats. Understandably bitter in 1970, when his reputation was at its lowest ebb, he replied when asked about the decline of his most famous novel:

I haven't read Lord of the Flies for fifteen years and I've forgotten it. The only point (historically) I'd like to make is that university students of the years '56 onward pushed the book on their professors who then had to teach it. The first flicker of student revolt? You tell me. Interestingly enough, those students are now teaching High School where my readership is so that I get a rivulet of letters from: professors writing books: post graduate students writing dissertations: High School students asking questions of understandable naivete. I dread to think of the next development—either complete neglect or "Dear Mr. Golding, my little Johnny is cutting his teeth on your Lord of the Flies and it gives him a pain in his poor little tummy. Could you write another book that doesn't give poor little babies pains in their poor little tummies?[10]

Golding has always been naive about American education; the situation was the reverse of what he described: it was the teachers who pushed the book on their students. It would certainly say something for the power of literature if a novel had fanned the flames of revolt!

"*Ritorna vincitor!*"

That Golding returned to favor in the 1980s suggests that the same set of circumstances that brought him to fame two decades earlier had recurred. Watergate inspired a heightened sense of morality, and the pendulum swung back to a 1950s-style conservatism. It is not coincidental that *Lord of the Flies* has been called the conservative's answer to the (liberal) *Catcher in the Rye*.[11] Similarly, *Darkness Visible* was the conservative's answer to the Age of Aquarius when a demythologized world took refuge in camp and comic strip characters, Pop Art and Op Art, happenings and street theatre, sit-ins, teach-ins, and love-ins, all of which confirmed Rollo May's thesis that loss of myth is a sign of a dying culture.

Since *Darkness Visible* is in many respects an indictment of the 1960s, it would have had no impact had it been published in 1969 when it would probably have been dismissed as the rantings of a Jeremiah. Ten years later when hindsight was possible, Golding's wisdom could be appreciated. In 1979 a character like Sim Goodchild in *Darkness Visible* could legitimately inveigh against the young who were willing to tear down a society to achieve the freedom they already had, and who were willing to dissent without knowing from what they were dissenting: "Those lovely creatures—they have everything—everything in the world, youth, beauty, intelligence—or is there nothing to live for? Crying out about freedom and justice! What freedom? What justice? Oh my God!" (259).

In *Darkness Visible,* Golding offers an Aeschylean explanation of the sixties' infatuation with violence, attributing it to boredom bred of indifference and lovelessness and manifesting itself in anomie and self-love. The two are interrelated; narcissism, which leads to nothing outside the self, draws one deeper into the self until, to escape from nothingness, it explodes in acts so meaningless that they can in no way be considered political.

Unlike Sophy, who withdrew so deeply into herself that she had only tunnel vision, by the end of the seventies Golding broke out of his cocoon and emerged into the twentieth century. *A Moving Target* (1982) made it clear that he had descended from his lofty perch atop the spire and was now down on earth, surveying the human landscape from eye level. Although the essays in *A Moving Target* are divided into Ideas and Places, they should be read consecutively, for Golding planned the collection as he would a book.

At first the book gives a feeling of déjà vu. "Wiltshire," the opening piece, had appeared in 1966; the next, "An Affection for Cathedrals," a year earlier. Then one sees the connection: the cathedral is the one in Salisbury, in Wiltshire where Golding lives. The cathedral was the model for the one in *The Spire,* the novel that, for Golding, was a beginning and an end. The two essays, then, are self-reflexive, pointing to Golding's past and the novel that encapsulated it. *The Spire* is the most perfect evocation of classical tragedy in contemporary fiction; yet it is a novel that could neither be surpassed nor duplicated. It ended the first phrase of Golding's career, and his twenty-year hibernation among the Greeks.

The third and fourth essays are reprints, travel articles written for *Holiday* magazine. Typical of Golding's travel pieces of the 1960s, they are gracefully written reminiscences, but the emphasis is on geography rather than humanity; as if the traveler had seen only sights, not people. The fifth essay, "Egypt from My Inside," was also a reprint from *The Hot Gates,* Golding's first collection of essays. Just when it seems that *A Moving Target* is a self-retrospective, an order appears: "Egypt from My Inside" is balanced by "Egypt from My Outside," the first original essay in the book. "Egypt from My Inside" was written from the perspective of a schoolboy seeing his first hieroglyphic and mummy case; it ends on a confessional note as Golding, the most Hellenic of novelists, boasts of his kinship with the ancient Egyptians: "I am in fact an ancient Egyptian, with all their unreason, spiritual pragmatism and capacity for ambiguous and even contradictory belief."[12]

The two essays are juxtaposed not merely because they deal with Egypt or because they are complementary, but because the second is a response to the first. One came from the imagination; the other, from experience. When Golding wrote the first piece, he had never been to Egypt; the experience and declaration of affinity were internal. Between 1964 and 1976, Golding went from a man of theory to a man of practice, from a storybook Egyptologist to a genuine tourist. The second Egypt essay is not an awestruck meditation on an exotic land, but a portrait of a country where one hotel has a bed in the lobby and another, a room with a balcony; where pregnant slaves trek through the sand after their masters as archaeologists dig up the past. In 1976, Golding discovered that Egypt was part of the Third World.

Just when it seemed that Golding had said all he wanted to say about Egypt, he came out with *An Egyptian Journal* (1985), his first work of nonfiction—*The Hot Gates* and *A Moving Target* being collections of essays. Apart from his publishers' desire for a full-length travel book, Golding had no pressing reason to write on a subject on which he had already expressed himself. Coincidentally, a third piece on Egypt, "In the Realm of Osiris," appeared in the *New York Times Magazine* on 6 October 1985 just as *An Egyptian Journal* arrived in the bookstores. Comparisons were inevitable. Golding's best travel essays were brief and congenially written, sometimes with a wit so dry that it fails to ignite but always with a touch of self-deprecating humor that humanizes what would otherwise have been a geographical exercise. The essay form reveals Golding's strengths: an informality that belies its depth, and a style that, while it never denies that a moral will be drawn, at least never becomes homiletic. Nothing in *An Egyptian Journal* forces the reader into introspection the way the end of "In the Realm of Osiris" does when Golding sums up his visit to the Valley of the Kings as a confrontation with "preoccupied selfishness."

A writer like Golding who prunes his style of excess and his narrative of repetitiveness should not adopt a diary format. The diurnal structure of *An Egyptian Journal* is irritating because too many of the events recorded do not warrant attention; although the striking photographs afford some relief, they do not conceal the fact that Golding is out of his element. A seasoned travel writer might have made something out of a Nobel Prize winner and his wife's being the only non-Egyptians on a boat going up the Nile; the experience itself might have yielded a magazine piece on culture shock. Although Golding must have edited the journal and polished up the writing before submitting it to Faber and Faber, it is still too much of a log and too little of the reflective memoir it should have been. Only once does the real Golding appear. It is not accidental that when Golding ceases being a voyager absorbing more than he can possibly communicate, he produces his best writing. As the boat nears Oxyrhynchus, the site of one of the most important papyri discoveries in the history of classical scholarship, Golding recalls how, as a boy, he always dreamed of finding manuscripts. Egypt's timelessness has affected him; he thinks back not to his actual, but to his archetypal, boyhood, wondering how Golding the boy would have fared in ancient Egypt since Golding the man is afraid of visiting modern Oxyrhynchus because it is dangerous. If the boy's behavior in Memphis on the day of the dead is any indication, he would have done just what the man did: he would have fled back to the boat. The child is indeed the father of the man.

An Egyptian Journal, however, corroborates what *A Moving Target* reveals about Golding: he was no longer spending his days studying E.R. Dodds's edition of the *Bacchae* or feasting on the "meat" of Greek literature. When Golding first came to prominence, he struck readers and critics as an erudite, but not especially literary, author. If he was widely read, he was not showing it. He seemed to be someone who read selectively, admitting he had not read the existentialists, Freud, and Conrad although critics found similarities to them in his work. Hence the surprise to find Golding in *A Moving Target* not only talking about poetry and fiction, but also about poets and novelists.

Since Golding writes with such ease and clarity, the reader may be tempted to confuse felicity of expression with lack of depth. In "Rough Magic," a comparison of fiction and drama, Golding seems to be stating the obvious by claiming that in drama people pretend to be others while in fiction they do not. It becomes apparent that what Golding means is that a novel is a single person's creation, unlike a play, which requires a writer, a director, a producer, a cast, and a set. The novelist is director, actor, set designer, and, ultimately, God. Golding could have made the customary distinction between interpretative and non-interpretative art, but that would have been too easy. He could also have invoked Aristotle's *Poetics* and argued for selective representation. This he does through his favorite trope, paradox. Fictional characters are unreal; they may come *from* life, but they are not *of* it.

Just when one thinks Golding is quibbling about prepositions, he does an about-face, and speaks about other popular novelists. He is himself, after all, one of them, and novelists never become popular by spouting theory, much less a prepositional theory of art. Golding proceeds to consider the problem of holding an audience (since he had lost it for more than a decade, he is extremely conscious of the issue); thus he contends that the novelist must "hook" or "get" the reader at the outset. To prove his point, he cites Hardy, Thackeray, Dickens, and Steinbeck. He illustrates the way Steinbeck makes a bid for the reader's attention at the beginning of *The Grapes of Wrath* by moving from the general to the particular, from the state of Oklahoma to its landscape— its roads, earth, and dust—until the central image, the dust bowl, is formed.[13]

Paradoxically, Golding's moving away from the classics made him more of a classicist; and his confrontation with the contemporary, while it encouraged him to explore sexuality more fully than he had in the past, deepened his religious sense. Thus he is led to link the novelist first with the saint and then with God. To Golding, the prototypical saint is John Mary Vianney, popularly known as the Curé of Ars; although uneducated, he had great powers of perception that enabled him to comprehend mysteries that elude and make sport of reason. The same ability, Golding maintains, is shared by great novelists.

Like the speaker in T. S. Eliot's "Ash Wednesday" who begs the Lady to teach him "to care and not to care," to be concerned but to be free of anxiety, Golding wants the novelist *not* to see so that he or she can see; to be silent in order to speak—but speak in a higher language that will not so much rearrange the world (that would be presumptuous) as to harmonize its dissonances. That would make the novelist more than a saint; it would make the novelist God, not in the sense of being able to manipulate characters or even create them, but of being able to enter a world that humankind shares with God—the world of the spirit, which eternalizes what comes from the world of the flesh. "The novelist is God of his own interior world," Golding affirms.[14] The novel enables the writer to understand finite creativity and at the same time share in God's creativity, which is infinite; the novel allows the writer, without recourse to Manicheanism or other forms of dualism, to perform the quintessential Godlike act: "to bring the disparate into equation."

This Golding has accomplished, and in his Nobel lecture, he came as close as he ever has in explaining how. Since the Swedish Academy expected a literary address that also did not ignore contemporary problems, Golding obliged by reconciling his theory of fiction with humanity's greatest fear: nuclear annihilation. To Golding, the novel is the paradigm of freedom because it allows readers to progress at their own pace, and the novelist to inhabit another's soul, dwelling there long enough to perform an act denied to the rest of humankind—the act of taking people out of obscurity and giving them life, thus preserving their individuality and dignity. Since the novelist is a life-bringer, the earth may erode, carcinogens multiply, wastes accumulate, and fish desert the coves of youth; but the novelist must go on reconciling present and past, life and death, fear of annihilation and belief in salvation so that, in the words of the mystic Juliana of Norwich, whom Golding admired as much as T. S. Eliot did, "all things will be well." To accomplish that goal, novelists must use the only means they have: language. Golding's mastery of that is the proof of what he preaches.

The Art with No Name

In his *New York Times* tribute to Golding, which appeared the day after he won the Nobel Prize, reviewer Anatole Broyard referred to the "author whose works defy normal labeling." Still, critics have tried to label them even though Golding's narrative form eludes definition. Kingsley Amis has termed Golding's novels science fiction, although his reasons (emphasis on ideas to the exclusion of naturalistic characterization, flashes of wit but no real humor, indifference to women and sex in general) are not especially compelling.[15] Yet there are still some who think of Golding as a sci fi writer, as the author discovered to his surprise after a lecture in Brisbane.

One reason some of Golding's work is mistaken for science fiction is that it is thought of as antiutopian. Golding, however, would argue to the contrary: the antiutopian wants to be proved wrong, yet Golding believes himself to be right about the human condition. Fable, a narrative that gives the impression of being preceded by the conclusion it is supposed to draw, is another common designation for Golding's fiction.[16] Golding has admitted that *Lord of the Flies* was the working out of a preconceived thesis; although the same probably applies to the other novels, that does not mean the author foresees his conclusions like a clairvoyant. Borrowing a phrase from scholastic metaphysics, Samuel Hynes calls the novels tropological in the Dantean sense; that is, formed along moral lines and embodying traditional ideas about human beings and their place in the universe.[17] In this context, the novels can be read as parables but of a particular kind: parables originating in personal experience. In *Varieties of Parable,* Louis MacNeice observes that writers of parables go back to their childhood—to their island, their sea, their dreams and nightmares, all of which furnish them with symbols for their moral tales. The essays show how certain incidents from Golding's life found their way into his art: a fear of darkness that he shares with Pincher Martin and Sammy Mountjoy; the quest for a bridge to span his world and his father's (*Free Fall*); youthful excavations that elicited compassion for prehistoric bones (*The Inheritors*); boyhood readings in Homer and Virgil that instilled in him a sense of the heroic (*The Spire*); service in the Royal Navy that gave him a firsthand knowledge of ships and seamen (*Pincher Martin, Rites of Passage*); the academics who descended on him—some to admire, some to use (*The Paper Men*).

Finally, there is Golding's dual label for his fiction: parody in the sense of using another's work as a point of departure, but with the qualifying "it-may-have-been-that way-then-but-not now"; and myth defined as "something that comes out from the root of things in the ancient sense of being the key to existence, the whole meaning of life, and experience as a whole."[18]

While all these designations are adequate, none is exact. When the Swedish Academy lauded Golding "for his novels which, with perspecuity of realistic narrative art and diversity and universality of myth, illuminate the world of today,"[19] it was acknowledging his extraordinary ability to harmonize opposites. Thus any classification of his fiction must be binary. Mythic allegory is the term that best characterizes Golding's work. Others (e.g., Eugene O'Neill, Jean Cocteau) have written mythic literature devoid of morality or moral literature devoid of myth (Henry James, Georges Bernanos, Graham Greene); Golding has written fiction in which myth and morality are one.

Implicit in every Golding novel is the fall, depicted as a subtext of images against which the narrative must be measured. In Golding, the fall is neither a dogma nor a motif; it is a concomitant of humanity that has been with the species as long as the species has been in existence. The fall, then is both mythic and allegorical; it is neither a parable of lost innocence nor a homily on the consequences of that loss, but both—a moral metaphor for humankind or, to use Golding's words, a "key to the mystery of existence." Golding renders human existence in terms of a tension between a conscious present and an unconscious past, the one supporting and giving rise to the other; to express that tension, he chooses a vehicle—an axis so geometrically conceived that, if it were to be visualized, it would look like a spindle around which the details and incidents spun by the author's imagination gather to form the narrative.

The Spire is an excellent example of the way Golding constructs an allegorical narrative. In Jocelin, one can see a line of questers from Oedipus to the western heroes of John Ford's epics, including Orestes, Parsifal and the Grail knights, Don Quixote, Faust, and Solness in Ibsen's *Master Builder*. Before Jocelin could enter the fourteenth century, he had to be purged of particularity, reduced to an archetype— the archetypal quester—to which Golding added flesh and substance. Golding starts with the soul; then he finds the soul a habitation. Since the soul is archetypal (that is, a primordial image), it shines forth through the body. Thus it can be seen in a variety of ways; the soul is capable of myriad reflections, while the body is totally singular. Jocelin, then, evokes every hero with a superhuman goal, but a goal that brings suffering and death as well as glory and fulfillment. Virgil's Aeneas was no different; he too had a divine mission: to found a new Troy and to bring the household gods of his people to Latium. For that mission to be accomplished, many lives had to be sacrificed: "So great a task it was to found the Roman race" (*Aeneid* 1.33). Aeneas brings tragedy wherever he goes—to Dido in Carthage, to Turnus in Italy; such is the paradox of the hero who carries out the divine will. Jocelin also has a mission that brings suffering and death. A dean's vision of capping his cathedral with a spire does not differ essentially from an exile's desire to find a homeland for his people. For the spire to be built, some must die; for a Troy to be established on Italian soil, the original inhabitants must be killed or assimilated. The only question is a moral one: was it worth it? As a novelist, Golding poses the question; he does not answer it.

The Spire, therefore, is mythic allegory; whether the fall is the central metaphor or whether it interpenetrates others (as it does in *The Spire* where it reinforces Jocelin's quest, which he envisions as a burgeoning apple tree with a serpent in it), it still points to a purpose beyond itself: "to speak of the things of God," as St. Augustine said and as Golding would concur. This is allegory, but allegory need not illuminate the contemporary world but only the soul of humankind. It was Golding's ability to do both, as the Swedish Academy realized, that merited him the Nobel Prize. Had he remained a Salisbury recluse, blending realism and myth and hermetically allegorizing, he would have become another visionary like Charles Williams or Paul Claudel. Golding, however, uses myth and allegory to create a double-profiled portrait of humankind—a Dionysian Apollo, achieving something that the Greeks could not: the simultaneous wearing of both masks; not just donning one and doffing the other (which would be wonderfully simple) but of altering the angle so that, at times, one is more conspicuous than the other. In finding the right face for the twentieth century, the right objective correlative, Golding has brought the disparate into equation. While he would be the last to expect to be canonized for his achievement, he would probably not deny it was worthy of a Nobel Prize.

Notes and References

Chapter One

1. Frederick L. Gwynn and Joseph L. Blotner, eds. *Faulkner in the University* (New York: Vintage Books, 1965), 4.
2. Bernard F. Dick, "'A Novelist Is a Displaced Person': An Interview with William Golding," *College English* 26 (March 1965): 480.
3. "My First Book," in *A Moving Target*, rev. ed. (New York: Farrar Straus Giroux, 1984), 147.
4. "The Ladder and the Tree," in *The Hot Gates and Other Occasional Pieces* (New York: Harcourt, Brace & World, 1966), 168.
5. See Cecil W. Davies, "The Novels Foreshadowed: Some Recurring Themes in Early Poems by William Golding," *English* 17 (1969): 86–89.
6. "The Writer in His Age," a reply to a questionnaire, in *London Magazine*, May 1957, 4.
7. Douglas A. Davis, "A Conversation with Golding," *New Republic*, 4 May 1963, 28.
8. Ibid., 30.
9. "It's a Long Way to Oxyrhynchus," *Spectator*, 7 July 1961, 9.
10. James Baker, *William Golding, A Critical Study* (New York: St. Martin's Press, 1965), xvii.

Chapter Two

1. Robert Michael Ballantyne, *The Coral Island* (London: 1858), 25–26. Subsequent references in the text are to this edition.
2. "The Meaning of It All," *Books and Bookmen*, October, 1959, 10. For parallels between Ballantyne and Golding, see Carl Niemeyer, "The Coral Island Revisited," *College English*, 22 (January 1961): 241–45.
3. *Lord of the Flies* (New York: Capricorn Books, 1959), 12. Subsequent references in the text are to this edition.
4. Euripides, *Bacchae*, ed. with introduction and commentary by E. R. Dodds, 2d ed. (London: Oxford University Press, 1960). Golding knew this edition "better than [his] own hand."
5. For the Euripidean influence, see Bernard F. Dick, "*Lord of the Flies* and the *Bacchae*," *Classical World*, 57 (January 1964): 145–46; Robert J. White, "Butterfly and Beast in *Lord of the Flies*," *Modern Fiction Studies* 10 (Summer 1964): 163–70.
6. "The Meaning of It All," 10. Golding's explanation is, however, quite sensible: "Now, look, I have a view which you haven't got and I would

like you to see this from my point of view. Therefore, I must first put it so graphically in my way of thinking that you identify with it, and then at the end I'm going to put you where you are, looking at it from the outside."

7. Dick, "'A Novelist Is a Displaced Person,'" 481.

8. James R. Baker, "An Interview with William Golding," *Twentieth Century Literature* 28 (Summer 1982): 136.

9. E.L. Epstein, "Notes on *Lord of the Flies*," in *Lord of the Flies* (New York: Capricorn Books, 1959), 254.

10. Robert Graves, *The White Goddess: A Historical Grammar of Poetic Myth* (New York: Noonday Press, 1966), 448.

11. "Lord of the Campus," *Time*, 22 June 1962, 64.

12. "Fable," in *The Hot Gates*, 96.

Chapter Three

1. "The Meaning of It All," 10.

2. H.G. Wells, *The Outline of History* (Garden City, N.Y.: Garden City Publishing Co., 1929), 69–70.

3. "The Meaning of It All," 10.

4. John Pfeiffer, commentary on Randall White, "Rethinking the Middle/Upper Paleolithic Transition," *Current Anthropology* 23 (1982): 185.

5. Wayland Young, "Letter from London," *Kenyon Review*, 29 (Summer 1957): 479.

6. *The Inheritors* (New York: Harvest Books, 1955), 58. Subsequent references in the text are to this edition.

7. "Digging for Pictures," in *The Hot Gates*, 61–70. Subsequent references are in the text.

Chapter Four

1. *Pincher Martin* (New York: Capricorn Books, 1962), 11. Subsequent references in the text are to this edition.

2. William York Tindall, *James Joyce: His Way of Interpreting the Modern World* (New York: Evergreen Books, 1960), 102.

3. Aeschylus, *Prometheus Bound*, 1043 ff., trans. E. A. Havelock, in *Eight Great Tragedies*, ed. Sylvan Barnet, Morton Berman, and William Burton (New York: Mentor Books, 1957), 51–52.

4. "Pincher Martin," *Radio Times*, 21 March 1958, 8.

Chapter Five

1. *Free Fall* (New York: Harbinger Books, 1960), 5. Subsequent references in the text are to this edition.

2. Chiefly Mark Kinkead-Weekes and Ian Gregor, *William Golding: A Critical Study*, rev. ed. (London: Faber & Faber, 1984), 165–99.

3. *New York Times,* 7 October 1983, sec. C, 20.
4. Ian Gregor and Mark Kinkead-Weekes, "The Strange Case of Mr. Golding and His Critics," *Twentieth Century,* February 1960, 120.
5. "All or Nothing," *Spectator,* 24 March 1961, 410.
6. "Thinking as a Hobby," *Holiday,* August 1961, 8, 13.
7. "On the Crest of the Wave," *Times Literary Supplement,* 17 June 1960, 387.
8. James Baker, *William Golding,* 94, n.5.

Chapter Six

1. See William Dodsworth, *An Historical Account of the Episcopal See and Cathedral Church of Sarum, or Salisbury* (Salisbury: 1814), 153.
2. "An Affection for Cathedrals," in *A Moving Target,* 17.
3. Lillian Feder, *Ancient Myth in Modern Poetry* (Princeton, N.J.: Princeton University Press, 1971), 10–11.
4. *The Spire* (New York: Harvest Books, 1964), 3. Subsequent references in the text are to this edition.

Chapter Seven

1. "The Anglo–Saxon," *Queen,* 22 December 1959, 27–30. This is the sole source of this story. Subsequent references are in the text.
2. The radio plays are unpublished and can be read only at the Scripts Library of the BBC, London.
3. "Miss Pulkinhorn," *Encounter,* August 1960, 27–32.
4. "Inside a Pyramid," *Esquire,* December, 1966, 300.
5. "On the Escarpment," *Kenyon Review* 29 (June 1967): 311.
6. Dennis Donoghue, "The Ordinary Universe," *New York Review of Books,* 7 December 1967, 21.
7. Baker, "Interview," 153. Don Crompton, *A View from the Spire: William Golding's Later Novels* (London: Blackwell, 1985), 58, accepts this statement but goes beyond it in his analysis.
8. *The Pyramid* (New York: Harcourt, Brace & World, 1967), 3. Subsequent references in the text are to this edition.
9. I made this point earlier in *"The Pyramid:* Mr. Golding's 'New' Novel," *Studies in the Literary Imagination* 2 (1969): 89.

Chapter Eight

1. *The Scorpion God* (London: Faber & Faber, 1971). "Envoy Extraordinary" published previously in *Sometime Never* (London: Eyre & Spottiswoode, 1956).
2. *The Brass Butterfly* (London: Faber & Faber, 1958).

Chapter Nine

1. Cecil Davis, "The Burning Bird: Golding's *Poems* and the Novels," *Studies in the Literary Imagination* 13 (1980): 114, shows how Golding's last poem about the phoenix ("the burning bird") with its reference to "mateless Beauty" contains the seeds of the purgation and resurrection imagery and the origin of Matty's name in *Darkness Visible*.
2. *Darkness Visible* (London: Faber Paperbacks, 1980), 37. Subsequent references in the text are to this edition.
3. Don Crompton first explained the allusion in "Biblical and Classical Metaphor in *Darkness Visible,*" *Twentieth Century Literature* 28 (1982): 200; see also Crompton, *A View from the Spire*, 102.
4. On the infernal wheel, see D. D. R. Owen, *The Vision of Hell: Infernal Journeys in Medieval French Literature* (New York: Barnes & Noble, 1971).
5. Joseph Campbell, *The Masks of God: Creative Mythology* (New York: Viking, 1970), 503.

Chapter Ten

1. *Rites of Passage* (New York: Playboy Paperbacks, 1982), 101. Subsequent references in the text are to this edition.
2. Baker, "Interview," 165.
3. Virginia Tiger, "William Golding's 'Wooden World': Religious Rites in *Rites of Passage,*" *Twentieth Century Literature* 28 (1982): 226.
4. Leonard Foster, "Translation: An Introduction," in *Aspects of Translation: Studies in Communication* (London: London University Research Center, 1951), 1.

Chapter Eleven

1. *"Gradus ad Parnassum,"* in *The Hot Gates*, 156.
2. *The Paper Men* (New York: Farrar, Straus & Giroux, 1984), 26. Subsequent references in the text are to this edition.

Chapter Twelve

1. "The 1983 Nobel Prize in Literature," *Dictionary of Literary Biography Yearbook: 1983* (Detroit: Gale Research Co., 1984), 12.
2. Ibid.
3. "Nobel Lecture 1983," in *A Moving Target*, 214.
4. The British study guides are worth owning, especially Graham Handley's in the Pan Study Aids series.
5. *"Lord of the Flies* Goes to College," *New Republic*, 4 May 1963, 27.
6. R. C. Townsend, "Lord of the Flies: Fool's Gold?" *Journal of General Education* 16 (July 1964): 160.

7. Kenneth Rexroth, "William Golding," *Atlantic Monthly*, May 1965, 96.

8. James R. Baker, "The Decline of *Lord of the Flies*," *South Atlantic Quarterly* 69 (1970): 448.

9. Ibid., 450.

10. Letter to author, 22 April 1970.

11. Francis E. Kearns, "Salinger and Golding: Conflict on the Campus," *America*, 26 January 1963, 136–39.

12. "Egypt from My Inside," in *A Moving Target*, 55.

13. "Rough Magic," in *A Moving Target*, 134.

14. "Belief and Creativity," in *A Moving Target*, 200.

15. Kingsley Amis, *New Maps of Hell* (New York: Ballantine Books, 1960), 24.

16. See John Peter, "The Fables of William Golding," *Kenyon Review* 19 (Autumn 1957): 577–92.

17. Samuel Hynes, *William Golding*, Columbia Essays on Modern Writers (New York: Columbia University Press, 1964), 5–6.

18. "The Meaning of It All," 9.

19. "The 1983 Nobel Prize in Literature," *Dictionary of Literary Biography Yearbook: 1983*, 12.

Selected Bibliography

PRIMARY SOURCES

1. Novels

Darkness Visible. London: Faber & Faber, 1979. Reprint. New York: Farrar, Straus & Giroux, 1979; London: Faber Paperbacks, 1980.

Free Fall. London: Faber & Faber, 1959. Reprint. New York: Harcourt, Brace & World, 1962; New York: Harbinger Books, 1962.

The Inheritors. London: Faber & Faber, 1955. Reprint. New York: Harcourt, Brace & World, 1962; New York: Harvest Books, 1963.

Lord of the Flies. London: Faber & Faber, 1954. Reprint. New York: Coward-McCann, 1955; New York: Capricorn Books, 1959.

The Paper Men. London: Faber & Faber, 1984. Reprint. New York: Farrar, Straus & Giroux, 1984; New York: Harvest Books, 1985.

Pincher Martin. London: Faber & Faber. 1956. Reprint. *The Two Deaths of Christopher Martin.* New York: Harcourt, Brace & World, 1957; New York: Capricorn Books, 1962.

The Pyramid. London: Faber & Faber, 1967. Reprint. New York: Harcourt, Brace & World, 1967.

Rites of Passage. London: Faber & Faber, 1980. Reprint. New York: Farrar, Straus & Giroux, 1980; New York: Playboy Paperbacks, 1982.

The Scorpion God: Three Short Novels. London: Faber & Faber, 1971. Reprint. New York: Harcourt Brace Jovanovich, 1972.

The Spire. London: Faber & Faber, 1964. Reprint. New York: Harcourt, Brace & World, 1964; New York: Harvest Books, 1964.

2. Nonfiction

An Egyptian Journal. London: Faber & Faber, 1985.

3. Essays

The Hot Gates and Other Occasional Pieces. London: Faber & Faber, 1965. Reprint. New York: Harcourt, Brace & World, 1966.

A Moving Target. London: Faber & Faber, 1982. Reprint. New York: Farrar, Straus & Giroux, 1983. Rev. ed. New York: Farrar, Straus & Giroux, 1984.

4. Play

The Brass Butterfly. London: Faber & Faber, 1958. Reprint in *The Genius of the Later English Theatre,* ed. Sylvan Barnet, Morton Berman, and William Burto. New York: New American Library/Mentor Books, 1962; London: Faber & Faber, 1963. (Faber school edition with introduction by author.)

5. Poetry

Poems. London: Macmillan & Co. 1934. Reprint. New York: Macmillan Co. 1935.

6. Stories

"The Anglo-Saxon." *Queen,* 22 December 1959.
"Envoy Extraordinary." In *Sometime Never: Three Tales of Imagination by William Golding, John Wyndham, and Mervyn Peake.* London: Eyre & Spottiswoode, 1956. Reprint. New York: Ballantine Books, 1962; In *The Scorpion God* (London: Faber & Faber, 1971).
"Inside a Pyramid." *Esquire,* December 1966.
"Miss Pulkinhorn." *Encounter,* August 1960.
"On the Escarpment." *Kenyon Review,* June 1967.

7. Unpublished Works (Radio Plays)

Break My Heart. British Broadcasting Corporation Third Programme, 19 March 1961.
Miss Pulkinhorn. British Broadcasting Corporation Third Programme, 20 April 1960.

SECONDARY SOURCES

Babb, Howard S. *The Novels of William Golding.* Columbus: Ohio State University Press, 1970. Lucidly written but tentative.
Baker, James R. *William Golding: A Critical Study.* New York: St. Martin's Press, 1965. The first critical study of Golding. Scholarly and readable.
———. "The Decline of *Lord of the Flies.*" *South Atlantic Quarterly* 69 (1970): 446–60. Attributes decline to the mood of the 1960s (Vietnam, Aquarianism, naive view of humanity, rejection of original sin).
Crompton, Don. *A View from the Spire: William Golding's Later Novels.* Edited and completed by Julia Briggs. New York: Blackwell, 1985. One of the finest books on Golding, left unfinished by the author's death.

Dick, Bernard F. "'The Novelist Is a Displaced Person': An Interview with William Golding." *College English* 26 (March 1965): 480–82. Golding on poetry, Freud, and Greek tragedy.

Dixon, M. E. *Brodie's Notes on William Golding's "The Spire."* London: Pan Books, 1978. Although called a "guide to exam success," it is a cut above the typical study guide. Sound criticism.

Epstein, E. L. "Notes on *Lord of the Flies.*" In *Lord of the Flies,* 249–55. New York: Capricorn Books, 1959. Biographical sketch plus some criticism including the "Oedipal wedding night" interpretation of the pigsticking.

Gindin, James. "'Gimmick' and Metaphor in the Novels of William Golding." *Modern Fiction Studies* 6 (Summer 1960): 145–52. Reprint. in *Postwar British Fiction.* Berkeley: University of California Press, 1962. The ending of each of the first four novels "palliates the force and unity of the original metaphor." Although "gimmick" is an unfortunate term, Golding himself used it vis-à-vis his first three novels (but not with respect to *Free Fall*).

Green, Peter. "The World of William Golding." *Review of English Studies* 1 (April 1960): 62–72. One of the first serious articles on Golding and still valid.

Gregor, Ian, and Mark Kinkead-Weekes. *William Golding: A Critical Study.* London: Faber & Faber, 1967. Reprint. New York: Harcourt, Brace & World, 1968. Revised 1984 to include chapter on *Darkness Visible* and *Rites of Passage,* some of which had appeared as an article in the Golding issue of *Twentieth Century Literature* 28 (Summer 1982). Thorough, sometimes exasperatingly so (the quotations tend to be excessive). One wishes for more complete footnotes and a bibliography.

Handley, Graham. *Brodie's Notes on William Golding's "Lord of the Flies."* London: Pan Books, 1976. Good insights into the way British class consciousness operates in the novel.

Hynes, Samuel. *William Golding.* Columbia Essays on Modern Writers. 2d ed. New York: Columbia University Press, 1968. Somewhat nebulous on Golding as a fabulist but convincing on *The Spire.*

Kermode, Frank. "The Novels of William Golding." *International Literary Annual* (1961): 11–29. Reprint. in *Puzzles and Epiphanies.* New York: Chilimark Press, 1962. An early appreciation by a critic who has remained one of Golding's staunchest admirers.

———, and William Golding. "The Meaning of It All." *Books and Bookmen* 5 (October 1959): 9–10. Unscripted discussion taken from BBC broadcast on 28 August 1959. Golding on Ballantyne, Wells, "gimmick," and the damning of Pincher Martin.

MacLure, Millar. "Allegories of Innocence." *Dalhousie Review* 40 (Summer 1960): 145–56. Although not exclusively on Golding (Faulkner and Camus are also included), this strangely neglected essay sensibly approaches innocence as something not remembered but merely believed.

Niemeyer, Carl. "The Coral Island Revisited." *College English* 22 (January 1961): 241–45. Shows Golding's use of Ballantyne without overstating the case. Golding quotes part of this essay in "Fable," *The Hot Gates*, 88–89.

Oldsey, Bernard S.and Stanley Weintraub. *The Art of William Golding.* New York: Harcourt, Brace & World, 1965. A highly literary study that puts Golding's fiction into proper perspective through a judicious choice of analogies.

Peter, John. "The Fables of William Golding." *Kenyon Review* 19 (Autumn 1957): 577–92. The first important critical essay on Golding in America (and one that he especially liked): notable for distinction between "fable" and "fiction."

White, Robert J. "Butterfly and Beast in *Lord of the Flies.*" *Modern Fiction Studies* 10 (Summer 1964): 163–70. A symbolic reading hinging on "butterfly" as a spiritual symbol.

Whitley, John S. *Golding: "Lord of the Flies."* London: Edward Arnold, 1970. A sophisticated study guide in the Studies in English Literature series whose editor is David Daiches.

Tiger, Virginia. *William Golding: The Dark Fields of Discovery.* London: Calder & Boyars, 1974. The novels through *The Scorpion God.* Exhaustive bibliography. Since the notes are as insightful as the text, they should not be overlooked.

Twentieth Century Literature 28 (Summer 1982). Special Golding issue containing James R. Baker's highly informative interview with the author and some outstanding criticism, especially by Don Crompton and Virginia Tiger.

Index